Journal of Ethnic Microhistory

Issue 12, II-2025

CONTENTS

Alex Dreger

Austro-Hungarian and German Newspapers about the Alexander Kuprin's Opinion on the Russian Army and the Revolution

Dipl.-Hist. Alex Dreger
Ausbildungs- und Forschungszentrum ETHNOS e.V.
Graduate historian Alex Dreger
Training and Research Center ETHNOS,
registered Association

Abstract

The author reviews the article "The Russian Army and the Revolution" (original German title: "Die russische Armee und die Revolution") anonymously published in "Dortmund Daily" (Dortmunder Tageblatt) on 24 September 1906. The analytical essay was placed on the front page of the newspaper released daily in provincial Dortmund and devoted to the examination of the novel "The Duel" by the Russian writer Alexander Kuprin (1870–1938). Dipl.-Hist. Alex Dreger is of the opinion that it was not surprising because at the beginning of the 20th century Russia bordered Germany in the east. Their relations were very complicated, especially after the Russia's defeat in the Russo-Japanese War (1904–1905). Russia was increasingly falling under the influence of Great Britain, which, in order to create an anti-German coalition, had entered into a rapprochement with France and Russia. In addition, the first Russian revolution (1905–1907) was raging in the empire, the outcome of which could have greatly changed the balance of power in European and world politics.

Alex Dreger argues that the officer corps acted as a stabilizing factor in the country's domestic policy. At the same time, the negativity with which A. Kuprin treats the officer corps, taking into account all those realities, seems short-sighted and biased. The Russian Armed Forces were perhaps one of the most obvious examples of how the country's defence needs often represented the sole driving force behind the state's development. They contributed to the great geographical discoveries, conquering Siberia and reaching the shores of the Pacific Ocean and the East Siberian Sea. Under Peter I, industry was created in the Urals for the needs of the army, and the newly created fleet went to Madagascar, Chukotka and Alaska.

Relative order and peacefulness were needed to substantiate the reforms in Russia. Without Russia's participation in the First World War, the country would have been able to stretch out the transformations over time, but the revolution happened at the very height of the global carnage and became a prologue to further upheavals that radically changed Russia and cost the lives of tens of millions of people.
Keywords: *Alexander Kuprin | Russian Army | the first Russian revolution (1905–1907) | Dortmunder Tageblatt | Russo-Japanese War | officer corps | First World War*

The "Dortmund Daily"[1] of 24 September 1906 published an article entitled "The Russian Army and the Revolution",[2] which examined a publication in one of the Viennese newspapers dedicated to the novel "The Duel" by the Russian writer Alexander Kuprin.[3]

Descendant of the Tatar Murza, Russian writer Alexander Ivanovich Kuprin (1870–1938)

From today's perspective, it is surprising not only that there was a response to an article concerning domestic Russian issues, but also that the publication was placed on the front page of a newspaper edited daily in a large industrially developed, but still provincial city. Nevertheless, the reasons for this are clear. At that time, Russia bordered Germany in the east. And their relations were very complicated, as they were increasingly aggravated by the countries being in hostile military alliances. The defeat in the Russo-Japanese War sharply narrowed the space for St. Petersburg's independent policy. Russia was increasingly falling under the influence of Great Britain, which, in order to create an anti-German coalition, had entered into a rapprochement with France and Russia. In addition, the first Russian revolution[5] was raging in the empire, the outcome of which could have greatly changed the balance of power in European and world politics.

Alexander Kuprin's novel expresses the author's critical attitude towards the negative phenomena in the Russian army and, to a certain extent, serves as a reflection of the view of the armed forces that prevailed in the bourgeois-liberal part of

Russian society. The fact that in his criticism A. Kuprin makes a reservation about the worst part of the officer corps in "uncultured and God-forsaken places" does not play a special role. Especially when the author adds that he is talking about the overwhelming majority of the Russian army.

How fair is the criticism of the author of "The Duel"? It is curious that the article in the "Dortmund Daily" passes over in eloquent silence the German equivalent of A. Kuprin's story. In 1903, the novel "Life In A Garrison Town"[6] by Fritz Oswald Bilse (1878–1951) was published, which described the daily life of the 16. Train-Battalion at Forbach in Lorraine. That is, in one of the least prestigious units of the German army, in a remote border province by the standards of that time. The reaction in society and the army practically repeated the reaction to "The Duel" in Russia. What made the scandal particularly piquant was that the author, Oswald Bilse, served in the unit in question. During the trial before the military court in Metz, it became clear that the young officer had not exaggerated the actual state of affairs. Despite this, he was sentenced to six months' imprisonment and dismissed from military service because of his defamation of the German Army Command. This only fueled the interest of the press, and the novel was banned in Germany, after which it began to be published in Vienna with the distribution of no less than one hundred thousand copies.[7]

So, the German reader of the article in "Dortmund Daily" did not at all perceive the fact that a Russian writer had exposed the Russian army as something impossible in the German army. The same contempt for civilians, the same impunity even in the case of murder for the most insignificant reason or without it.

In 1896, Lieutenant Henning von Brüsewitz[8] hacked a man to death in Karlsruhe after feeling insulted. The court sentenced him to three years and twenty days in prison, of which he served only half. The incident caused widespread public outrage, as did the Zabern incident[9] in 1913, when the Kaiser personally spared the outrageous military from punishment. And we are talking about the army that was considered, not without reason, the best in the world. Since the German Empire was a constitutional monarchy, many of the cases of abuse and violence in the army became the subject of hearings in the Reichstag.

As a result, the command did indeed strive to improve the situation – and not without some success, but nevertheless, it was not possible to completely correct it at that time, as, incidentally, it has not been possible to do so to this day in any mass army of the world. Chancellor Leo von Caprivi[10] in a speech before the Reichstag in 1892 came to the conclusion that such cases could not be completely eliminated, since "there are always rude and violent people".[11] Perhaps the Chancellor was right. In the case of the German army, one must not forget the high social prestige of the armed forces in society. After all, it was the Prussian army that made it possible to create the German Empire, providing two generations of Germans with peace and the opportunity for economic and civilizational development.

In 1906, the prestige of the armed forces fell after the defeat in a war with a relatively small Asian country, which was difficult for society to explain.

The revolution did not bypass the army and navy servicemen participated in the mutinies en masse, but it was the loyalty of the officer corps and the army that ultimately allowed not only to cope with the unrest in the armed forces, but also to suppress the uprisings in the cities and in the countryside. It is significant that in the entire navy there was only one officer who joined the rebels – Captain 2nd Rank Pyotr Petrovich Schmidt.[12] In his story, A. Kuprin makes predictions for the future based on the experience he had. Considering changes necessary, he sees two forces in the army – the officer corps and the soldier masses, who pursue opposing interests.

Officers act as forces of evil, reactionary in nature, rude and uneducated. Is it permissible to consider such an assessment or opposition of the officer corps to civilians, correct? The second part of the question is easy enough to answer. By the beginning of the 20th century, the officer corps of the Russian Imperial Army had long ceased to be a noble "reserve". It was dominated by people from the same strata of Russian society that made up its educated part. Accordingly, civil servants in the remote provinces suffered from the same ailments as their military colleagues. And there is a sea of evidence for this in Russian literature of that period.

Therefore, there is no reason to contrast the officer corps with civil society. Was the officer corps reactionary? This is a much more complex question. According to the regulations, an officer had no right to engage in political activity (in the realities of an autocratic monarchy, political activity was synonymous with anti-government activity) and swore allegiance to the emperor. Thus, the officer corps really acted as a stabilizing factor in the country's domestic policy. At the same time, the negativity with which A. Kuprin treats the officer corps, taking into account all those realities, seems short-sighted biased.

What the army prevented in 1905–1907[13] overtook the educated classes of the Russian society in 1917,[14] putting an end to both the illusions of the liberal intelligentsia and the physical existence of a significant part of it. At the same time, the specificity of the armed forces in any country is that they are consumers of the achievements of scientific and technical progress.

The Russian Armed Forces are perhaps one of the most obvious examples of how the country's defence needs often represented the sole driving force behind the state's development.

During the era of Ivan IV Vasilyevich,[15] a poor and otherwise economically weak country, not without the participation of foreign specialists, produced first-class artillery by the standards of that time in quantities comparable to the most developed countries of Europe.

The armed forces contributed to the great geographical discoveries, conquering Siberia, reaching the shores of the Pacific Ocean and the East Siberian Sea. Under Peter I, industry was created in the Urals for the needs of the army, and the newly created fleet went to Madagascar, Chukotka and Alaska.

Subsequently, a hydrometeorological service and the Russian Geographical Society were created to meet the needs of the fleet. The need for engineering personnel led to the creation of the Main Military Engineering School[16] in Saint Petersburg, just a few years after the establishment of a similar educational institution in France. Its graduates ensured the construction of not only fortifications, but also railways.

Maybe the most famous graduate of the Main Military Engineering School is Fyodor Mikhailovich Dostoevsky,[17] the son of a poor Moscow doctor; he was a more typical representative of school graduates than an exception to the rule. It is unlikely that the classic of Russian and world literature can be considered belonging to uneducated circles of the Russian society of that time. Russian literature received perhaps the best part of its writers and poets from the officer ranks.

The armed forces in Russia are intrinsically linked to the development of medicine. Against the backdrop of the undoubtedly weak health care in the country as a whole, imperial Russia could be proud of its achievements in military field surgery (Nikolay Ivanovich Pirogov[18]) and epidemiology.

Electricity during the Crimean War[19] was still a poorly researched exotic, but the approaches to Kronstadt[20] were already covered by minefields, the explosions of which were initiated by electricity. It is not surprising that the electric illumination of the coronation of Alexander II[21] in Moscow was carried out by officers of the Baltic Fleet – the country had no other specialists at that time.

The still disputed primacy in the discovery of radio is also associated with a naval officer – Alexander Stepanovich Popov.[22] The list can be continued up to the present time. Therefore, the actual generalization of the Russian officer corps in the negative guise of its individual representatives from remote garrisons cannot be considered justified.

The assertion that ordinary officers would flee at the first nearby explosion of an artillery shell is equally unfounded. To refute this slander, it is not at all necessary to look at the events of the Civil War.[23] The officers who returned from the Russo-Japanese War[24] were often involved in suppressing unrest. The Baltic provinces are a particularly typical example. Since they were the main source of formation of naval crews, officers who returned after Tsushima[25] led the suppression of uprisings in the region. Thus, the former flagship artilleryman Kurosh[26] was the only officer on the battleship Nikolai I[27] who spoke out against the surrender of the remnants of the squadron to the Japanese that was ordered by Rear Admiral Nebogatov.[28] At the same time, in the battle, the gunners of the Nikolai I, the oldest of the squadron's battleships, showed themselves to be very worthy, inflicting the most severe damage on the enemy. In retaliation for the suppression of the uprisings, the Socialist Revolutionaries stabbed to death his 12-year-old son, a grammar school pupil, in Riga.

After the battle at Tsushima, Captain 2nd Rank Richter[29] attempted to break away from two Japanese destroyers on the destroyer Bystry, but due to a lack of coal, he scuttled the ship, preventing its capture by the enemy. He also participated in the pacification of the Baltic region at the head of sailor detachments.

A. Kuprin has a special dislike for the guard. Remembering its role in the coups of the 18th century, the writer suspects the presence of a secret monarchist organization in its ranks. It is difficult to judge the validity of this assumption. The Semenovsky Regiment[30] played a decisive role in the battles with the rebels in Moscow in 1905.

However, in 1917, the Guard did not save the monarchy. Moreover, Grand Duke Kirill Vladimirovich[31] and his guards unit joined the rebels, like "Prince Egalite"[32] during the French Revolution. The Guard of 1917 was only a shadow of itself. The real Russian Guard, together with its officers, perished in Galicia[33] at the very beginning of World War I. Saint Petersburg housed reserve units that became the catalyst for workers' uprisings and ensured the success of the February Revolution.

Likewise, the mutiny in the navy affected only the brigade of new battleships in Helsinki.

Their crews practically did not go to sea throughout the war, while the older ships in the Gulf of Riga maintained discipline and fought actively with the German fleet, which captured the islands of the Gulf of Riga during Operation Albion.[34]

It is interesting that in Germany, the collapse of the monarchy began with a naval revolt in Kiel, and not with army units suffering terrible losses at the front.

In conclusion, it is worth dwelling on the key idea of A. Kuprin: the government must meet the population halfway, without persecution and threats. The wish is, of course, good, but as usual – with simple answers to complex questions – impossible to fulfil.

Although Stolypin's reforms[35] began in the country, they could progress only after the eventuation of relative order and peacefulness in the country. Simultaneously these reforms revealed presence of contradictions that could not be resolved without shedding of much blood. Perhaps, without Russia's participation in the First World War, the country would have been able to stretch out the transformations over time, but the revolution happened at the very height of the global carnage and became a prologue to further upheavals that radically changed Russia and cost the lives of tens of millions of people.

The original text of the article in German

Stichwörter: *Alexander Kuprin | Novelle „Zweikampf" | russische Armee | Revolution | Offizierkorps | Klasseninteressen | Staatsduma*

36

Die russische Armee und die Revolution.

Von Alexander Kuprin,[37] einem ehemaligen hohen russischen Offizier und hervorragendem Vertreter des modernen russischen Schrifttums, dessen Militärroman "Zweikampf"[38] in Russland großes Aufsehen erregt hat und in alle europäischen Sprachen übersetzt wurde, der auch als Herausgeber der vornehmen, dieser Tage vom Stadthauptmann von Petersburg[39] ohne Angabe von Gründen verbotenen Monatsschrift „Mir Boschi"[40] in literarischen Kreisen bekannt geworden ist, brachte vor einiger Zeit die Wiener „Neue Freie Presse"[41] einen interessanten Artikel, in welchem der Verfasser ein gradezu trostloses Bild von den Zuständen im russischen Offizierkorps entwirft und die Stellung der Armee zur Revolution beleuchtet. Wir entnehmen dem Aufsatze die folgenden Ausführungen mit dem Bemerken, dass Kuprin seine Schilderung mit dem Vorbehalt einleitet, dass er bloß von den Offizieren in den noch völlig „unkultivierten und gottvergessenen Ortschaften" spreche; freilich bilden diese, wie er hinzufügt, die erdrückende Mehrheit der russischen Armee.

Den Dienst betrachten die Offiziere als ein unerträgliches, entsetzlich langweiliges Joch und wenden knabenhafte Mittel, wie Simulierung von Krankheit und heimliche Flucht vom Exerzierplatz, an, um sich ihm zu entziehen. In dem Soldaten erblicken sie ein verstecktes, elendes, listiges Tier, auf welches nur Schläge und Strafen einwirken können. Es gibt keine Disziplin, sondern Furcht und Servilismus. Ihre Zerstreuungen? Billiard, Karten, Schnaps, Mädchen, Branntwein und Branntwein. Was lesen sie? Absolut nichts, wenn man nicht den „Russkij Invalid"[42] rechnet, wo nur Beförderungen gedruckt werden. Es bestehen kleine, fadenscheinige Regimentsbibliotheken. Die Unterleutnants entleihen noch zweimal im Jahre Boulevard-Romane, die Leutnants aber verschmähen sogar auch diese Literaturgattung. Militärische Werke werden gar nicht gelesen.

Wie verhalten sie sich zu den friedlichen Bürgern? Mit unerschütterlicher, großartigster Verachtung. Gelehrte, Schriftsteller, Professoren und Künstler sind in ihren Augen nichts als elende, minderwertige, zivilistische Kreaturen, ein „Gesindel" … Einen Zivilisten beleidigen, verprügeln, entehren, das kann man völlig straflos tun. Man darf hoch zu Ross in eine andersgläubige Kirche reiten, man darf in einer Synagoge eine Nauserei in betrunkenem Zustande veranstalten. Das sind nur Streiche. Man darf mit Hilfe von Soldaten die ganze jüdische Bevölkerung eines Städtchens der körperlichen Züchtigung unterwerfen. Das ist nur ein komischer Vorfall. Die Ermordung eines Zivilisten in einem Restaurant, auf einem Spaziergang oder in einem öffentlichen Lokal bleibt ungestraft, wenn man zwei oder drei Monate Haft nicht rechnet. Die Kameraden erblicken darin nur ein Bravourstück.

So ist unser Offizierkorps. Wie also kann es also auf die letzten Ereignisse und auf die Auseinandertreibung der Duma[43] reagieren? Selbstverständlich gar nicht. Es unterliegt keinem Zweifel, dass der größte Teil der Reichsduma von der Petersburger Stadtduma (Stadtverwaltung) nicht zu unterscheiden weiß. Dabei muss noch hervorgehoben werden, dass der Durchschnittsoffizier von der Überzeugung durchdrungen ist, dass die Duma, dank den Machenschaften der Juden zusammengetreten ist, und dass ihre Mitglieder im Solde der Juden stehen. Was in der Duma geschah und was dort gesprochen wurde, davon hat er absolut keine Ahnung.

Wie verhält sich der Offizier zur Revolution? Gerade so. Er vermutet sie gar nicht. Wenn aber dunkle Gerüchte von der Revolution an sein Ohr dringen, so schlägt er die Hände zusammen, öffnet weit die Augen und sagt mit ungekünstelter Bewunderung: „Freiheit? Der Teufel soll sie holen, welche Freiheiten wollen sie noch? Und an allem haben die Studenten Schuld. Sie wollen nicht lernen, und deshalb rebellieren sie. Sie alle soll man unter die Soldaten stecken, die Arbeiter aber körperlich züchtigen!" Der Offiziere der Strafexpedition bemächtigt sich einer Arte Blutwahnsinn. Es genügt, hervorzuheben, dass diese Offiziere freiwillig die Pflichten eines Henkers übernehmen.

Etwas anders stehen die Dinge in der Gard. Dort hat man von der Freiheitsbewegung einen Begriff und man sieht ihren gefährlichen Umfang. Ich halte es deshalb für vollkommen sicher, dass unter den Gardetruppen sich durch eine Verschwörung ein geheimer Militärverband gebildet hat, welcher bereit war, aus eigener Initiative die gewaltsame, selbst blutige Schließung der Duma vorzunehmen. Dieser privilegierte Truppenteil, welcher aus der Blüte der adeligen Jugend besteht, scheint sich klar bewusst zu sein, dass er im Kampfe gegen die Volksfreiheit für seine Klasseninteressen kämpft.

Man mag fragen: Wäre es möglich, dass der Geist des Freiheitskampfes in die Armee gar nicht gedrungen ist? Ja, er ist dahin gedrungen. Aber der von der allgemeinen Bewegung ergriffene Offizier verbleibt nicht lange im Regiment. Die geistig entwickelten, ehrlich denkenden und bewussten Offiziere sind von selbst bestrebt, aus den erstickenden Katakomben dieser düsteren, grausam verwilderten und eingeschlossenen Kaste sich zu befreien. Und diese stellen die leidenschaftlichsten, kühnsten Revolutionäre. Es ist allgemein bekannt, dass in den Kasematten der Peter Pauls-Festung viele Offiziere eingekerkert sind. Es sind meistens Artilleristen und Sappeure, am wenigstens aber Infanteristen.

Was tut und denkt zur selben Zeit der Soldat? Unser Soldat, das ist unser Bauer. Während der ganzen Dauer des ersten Dienstjahres, so lange sein Heimweh nicht erloschen, ist er noch immer Bauer. Der Offizier ist allen und allem entfremdet: der Natur, dem Boden, der Gesellschaft, welche ihn geringschätzt und fürchtet, und in Wirklichkeit auch dem Vaterlande. Der Soldat aber, der seine Bauernseele nicht eingebüßt hat, ist durch seine Bande an das Volk geknüpft. Der Bauer gehorcht der Obrigkeit, er gehorcht aus längst vorhandener, jahrhundertelanger Furcht, aus Trägheit und aus Unverständnis. Ebenso verhält sich der Soldat seinem Offizier gegenüber. Volk und Armee stehen noch jetzt der Politik fern und beschämend gleichgültig der Freiheit gegenüber.

Man wird mir jedoch entgegen: „Wodurch soll man alle Schrecknisse der letzten Jahre erklären?" Ich wiederhole noch einmal: unsere Armee ist eine B a u e r n a r m e e. Die macht der Wirkung gleicht jener Gegenwirkung. Dieses unerbittliche Gesetzt bleibt Gesetz auch in der Geschichte. Nirgends hat Sklaverei und Vergewaltigung solche äußersten Grenzen erreicht wie in Russland im Laufe von Jahrhunderten. Und im Laufe dieser Jahrhunderte hat sich ein unermesslicher historischer Volkshass angesammelt, ohne zum Vorschein zu kommen, sondern sich mit jedem Jahre immer mehr entflammend. Der fast prophetische Dichter Puschkin[44] dachte mit Schrecken an jene Zeit, in welcher „ein russischer Aufstand sinnlos und unbarmherzig ausbrechen wird."[45] Nun, wir stehen am Vorabend eines solchen Aufstandes Armee und Volk stecken sich gegenseitig an und muntern sich gegenseitig auf. Wenn die Feuersbrunst die Armee ergreifen wird, wird sie auch die Bauernschaft ergreifen; wird die Explosion in der Bauernschaft erfolgen, so wird auch sie auch die Armee entzünden.

Wie wird es geschehen? Ich glaube, den Anfang wird die Armee machen, und zwar unbedingt mit der Unterdrückung eines bewaffneten Aufstandes der Parteirevolutionäre. Und nicht einen Augenblick darf daran gezweifelt werden, dass die zur Unterdrückung des Aufstandes ausrückenden Offiziere beim ersten trefflicheren Artillerieschuss die Flucht ergreifen werden. Und dieser erste Artillerieschuss wird das Signal sein zur allgemeinen, fast augenblicklichen Auflösung der Armee und zur Volkerhebung. – Wird es jemandem gelingen, diesen Lavastrom aufzuhalten? Große Zeiten erzeugen große Helden. Das russische Volk, welches Peter den Großen[46] geboren hat, kann auch einen neuen Napoleon erzeugen. Das wäre der ausgezeichnete Ausgang.

Es gibt aber, so schließt Kuprin, einen anderen Ausweg, einen friedlichen und sicheren. Die Regierung muss der Volksfreiheit die äußersten Konzessionen machen. Wir wissen nicht, wie die kommende Duma ausschauen wird. In Russland ist alles möglich: Die Duma kann reaktionär, gemäßigt und äußerst revolutionär ausfallen. Die Regierung muss aber begreifen, dass es für sie die höchste Zeit ist, von selbst den Bevölkerungsbedürfnissen entgegenzukommen, ohne Antreibung und Drohung. Einen anderen unblutigen Ausgang gibt es nicht: das ist der ganzen russischen Gesellschaft klar.

References and Explanations /
Referenzen und Erläuterungen

1. Dortmunder Tageblatt

2. Die russische Armee und die Revolution.

3. Aleksandr Ivanovich Kuprin (1870–1938) was a Russian writer. His father was Russian, his mother belonged to a noble Volga Tatar family. In 1880, inspired by Russia's victory in the Russo-Turkish War (1877–1878), Kuprin was enrolled into the Second Moscow Military High School, and turned over to the Cadet Corps in 1882. In the autumn of 1888, Kuprin left the Cadet Corps to enter the Alexander Military Academy in Moscow. In 1890, he graduated from the Academy ranked sublieutenant and was posted to the 46th Dnieper Infantry Regiment stationed in Proskurov (now Khmelnitsky), where he spent the next four years. Kuprin's years of military service saw the publication of several short stories, which finally resulted in his most famous work, "The Duel" (1905). After the 1905 Revolution Kuprin became openly critical of the regime. He established links with sailors of the Black Sea Fleet in Sevastopol, and even attempted to enlist on the battleship Potemkin, which mutinied in June 1905. As World War I broke out, Kuprin opened a military hospital in his home. As a reserve officer he was called up in November 1914, and commanded an infantry company in Finland till May 1915, when he was discharged on grounds of ill health. After the October Revolution (7 November 1917) Kuprin left for Finland and ultimately emigrated to France (1920) settling down in Paris. The years in Paris saw the decline of Kuprin's creativity and his succumbing to alcoholism. In late 1936, he finally decided to leave for Soviet Russia. The years in Paris had broken his health. Aleksandr Ivanovich Kuprin died on 25 August 1938.

4. https://greylib.align.ru/741/aleksandr-kuprin-tatarskie-korni.html; downloaded on 28 April 2025 at 21:00.

5. The Russian Revolution of 1905, also known as the First Russian Revolution, began on 22 January 1905 and led to the establishment of a constitutional monarchy under the Russian Constitution of 1906, the country's first. It was characterized by mass political and social unrest including worker strikes, peasant revolts, and military mutinies directed against Emperor Nicholas II and the autocracy, who were forced to establish the legislative assembly "State Duma" and grant certain rights.

Bugaboo of Revolution
Drawing by Boris Kustodiev, 1905
https://commons.wikimedia.org/wiki/
File:Жупел_революции.jpg

6. Bilse, Fritz Oswald: Aus einer kleinen Garnison / Ein militärisches Zeitbild. Wiener Verlag, Wien 1904.

7. Neitzel, Sönke: Deutsche Krieger / Vom Kaiserreich zur Berliner Republik – eine Militärgeschichte. Propyläen Verlag, Berlin 2020; ISBN: 978-3549076477; S. 48.

8. Henning von Brüsewitz (1862–1900), a first lieutenant in the 1st Baden Life Grenadier Regiment No. 109, killed the 31-year-old mechanic Theodor Siepmann in Karlsruhe on 11 October 1896, because he felt Siepmann had insulted him. The act and its lenient punishment led to heated debates about the concept of honour, caste mentality, militarism, and duelling in public and in the Reichstag.

9. The twenty-year-old Second Lieutenant Günter Freiherr von Forstner (1893–1915) spoke disparagingly about the inhabitants of Zabern (Alsace-Lorraine) on 13 October 1913 during a troop induction. He said to his soldiers, "If you are attacked, then make use of your weapon; if you stab such a Wackes in the process, then you'll get ten marks from me". (Wackes is a German derogatory term for a native Alsatian). The local newspapers informed the public about these events. The population protested strongly against this treatment by the Prussian military. The official statement of the authorities tried to play down the incident, and interpreted "Wackes" as a general description for quarrelsome people. The relationship between Alsace-Lorraine and the rest of the German Empire was noticeably affected for the worse because of that affair. The Alsatians and Lorrainers felt themselves more helplessly at the mercy of the arbitrariness of the German military than ever. Following the conduct of the military, the term "zabernism" found its way into the English language of the time as a description for the abuse of military authority or for tyrannical, aggressive conduct in general. (https://en.wikipedia.org/wiki/Zabern_Affair)

10. Leo von Caprivi (1831–1899) served as the Imperial Chancellor of the German Empire from March 1890 to October 1894. He abandoned Bismarck's military, economic, and ideological cooperation with the Russian Empire and failed to establish good relations with the United Kingdom of Great Britain and Ireland, though his administration pursued a pro-British foreign policy. Caprivi sought rapprochement with the French Third Republic.

11. Protokolle des Deutschen Reichstags. 8. Legeslaturperiode, 172. Sitzung, 15.2.1892, S. 4209.

12. Pyotr Petrovich Schmidt (1867–1906) was one of the leaders of the Sevastopol Uprising during the Russian Revolution of 1905. He was born to the family of rear admiral and the head of Berdyansk port, Pyotr Petrovich Schmidt (1828–1888). His mother was Yekaterina Yakovlevna Schmidt (born von Wagner). From 1880 to 1886, Schmidt studied at the St. Petersburg Naval School. In 1886, he was enlisted in the 8th naval crew as a midshipman. On 17 January 1888, he was assigned to the Black Sea Fleet.

Almost immediately, an unpleasant incident occurred. Being in a painful nervous attack, Schmidt came to the fleet commander's office and threw a tantrum, "saying all sorts of absurd things". After this Schmidt was urgently sent on a 6-month leave. This was followed by a series of leaves with rare breaks for service. He underwent treatment in a private hospital for the nervous and mentally ill in Moscow. In 1897, Schmidt was diagnosed with schizophrenia with delusions of grandeur.

Pyotr Petrovich Schmidt (1867–1906)
https://commons.wikimedia.org/
wiki/File:Schmidt_Petr.jpg

On 13 January 1889, Schmidt entered into an official marriage with a professional prostitute, which caused extreme abhorrence of him among the officers. His father, upon learning of what had happened, died suddenly.

In June 1905, he was in Odessa, which was engulfed in rebellion and unrest, and then a dark story with government money occurred. Schmidt took the ship detachment's cash (2,500 gold rubles) and went to Kyiv, where he lived in luxury. Schmidt was brought before a military court for embezzlement and desertion, but thanks to the intervention of his relatives, who paid off the money he had embezzled from their personal funds and arranged for him to be discharged from the navy on an urgent basis; the case was hushed up without consequences.

In August 1905, Schmidt returned to Sevastopol, where he conducted anti-government propaganda and organized the "Union of Officers – Friends of the People"; he was the sole member of that. On 25 October 1905, at a rally he suffered a seizure and convulsed in front of the crowd.

On October 31, Schmidt called on the crowd to free political prisoners from the Sevastopol city prison. The prison was under the protection of the garrison, so this call was evidently a provocation. Upon arrival at the prison, Schmidt demanded that the prison director release not only political prisoners but also criminal prisoners, to which he received a legally justified refusal. Then Schmidt called on the crowd to storm the prison, after which the people rushing to the gates were met by a volley of garrison soldiers; as a result, 8 people from the crowd were killed. On November 2, at a rally in honour of the eight people who died during the unsuccessful storming of the prison, he gave a speech that became known as the "Schmidt oath": "We swear that we will never concede to anyone a single inch of the human rights we have won". Afterwards, Schmidt had another nervous attack, and did not go to the cemetery where the dead were buried. Schmidt was arrested that same day. He was conveyed to the battleship "Tri Sviatitelia", which provoked protests and the authorities were forced to release him.

On the evening of November 13, a parliamentary commission consisting of sailors and soldiers delegated from various branches of the armed forces, including seven ships, invited retired naval lieutenant Schmidt, who had gained great popularity during the October rallies, to lead the military coup.

On November 27, he led a mutiny on the cruiser Ochakov and other ships of the Black Sea Fleet. Schmidt declared himself commander of the Black

Sea Fleet, giving the signal: "I command the fleet. Schmidt." On the same day, he sent a telegram to Russian Emperor Nicholas II: "The glorious Black Sea Fleet, sacredly devoted to the people, demands Your Majesty to immediately call a meeting of the Constituent Assembly, and no longer obeys orders of Your ministers. Commander of the Fleet P. Schmidt". The commander of the Imperial Russian forces, General Alexander Meller-Zakomelsky, gave the ultimatum demanding immediate capitulation, but there was no reply. Three hours after the ultimatum, the government forces opened fire at rebel ships and barracks. In 90 minutes, the revolutionary squadron was defeated by the government ships led by the battleship Rostislav. Schmidt and his 16-year-old son were captured, and all who remained alive were arrested. The next day, the government forces supported by artillery took the rebellion barracks.

A closed hearing was held in February 1906 Schmidt and other leaders of the uprising were sentenced to death. He was executed on 19 March 1906.

13. See reference 5.

14. The February Coup was the first of two revolutions, which took place in the Russian Imperium in 1917. It was provoked by military failures during the First World War. The main events of the revolution took place in Petrograd (now Saint Petersburg), the then-capital of the Russian Imperium, where long-standing discontent with the monarchy erupted into mass protests against food rationing on 23 February (Old Style) / 8 March (New Style) 1917. The Russian Provisional Government was formed and Emperor Nicholas II was forced to abdicate.

The October Revolution, which unfolded on 25 October (Old Style) / 7 November (New Style) 1917, was organized by the left-wing extremist Bolshevik party. It was not recognized by variety of social and political groups, who opposed the drastic restructuring championed by the Bolsheviks. The Russian Civil War, which broke out in the months following the revolution, resulted in the deaths and suffering of millions of people.

15. Ivan IV Vasilyevich (1530–1584) was Grand Prince of Moscow and all Russia from 1533 to 1547, and the first Tsar and Grand Prince of all Russia from 1547 until his death in 1584. His reign was characterised by Russia's transformation from a medieval state to an emergent empire. Ivan IV also revised the legal code and introduced reforms, including elements of local self-government, as well as establishing the first Russian standing army, the streltsy. Ivan IV conquered the khanates of Kazan and Astrakhan, and significantly expanded the territory of

Russia. He claimed not to be a "Russe" highlighting his "German" descent from Rurik who, according to tradition, was invited to reign in Novgorod in the year 862.

16. The Saint Petersburg Military Engineering School was founded in 1810. In 1819, it was renamed as the Main Military Engineering School.

17. Fyodor Mikhailovich Dostoevsky (1821–1881) was a Russian novelist, short story writer, essayist and journalist. He is regarded as one of the greatest novelists in both Russian and world literature. Dostoevsky entered the Main Military Engineering School in January 1838 and graduated from it in 1843. On 12 August 1843, Dostoevsky took a job as a lieutenant engineer.

18. Nikolay Ivanovich Pirogov (1810–1881) was one of the most widely recognized Russian physicians. Considered to be the founder of field surgery, he was the first to use anaesthesia in a field operation (1847) and one of the first surgeons in Europe to use ether as an anaesthetic. He is credited with the invention of various kinds of surgical operations and developing his own technique of using plaster casts to treat fractured bones.

19. The Crimean War was fought between the Russian Empire and an alliance of the Ottoman Empire, the Second French Empire, the United Kingdom of Great Britain and Ireland, and the Kingdom of Sardinia-Piedmont from October 1853 to February 1856.

20. Founded in the early 18th century by Peter the Great (1672–1725), Kronstadt became a primary maritime defence outpost of the Russian capital Saint Petersburg. The main base of the Russian Baltic Fleet was also located in Kronstadt, guarding the approaches to the capital city.

21. Alexander II (1818–1881) was Emperor of Russia, King of Poland and Grand Duke of Finland from 2 March 1855 until his assassination in 1881. His most significant reform was the emancipation of Russia's serfs in 1861, for which he is known as Alexander the Liberator.

22. Alexander Stepanovich Popov (1859–1906) was a Russian physicist who was one of the first people to invent a radio receiving device. He worked as a teacher at a Russian naval school. On 7 May 1895, Popov presented a paper on a wireless lightning detector he had built that worked via using a coherer to detect radio noise from lightning strikes. This day is celebrated today in Russia as Radio Day. In a 24 March 1896 demonstration, he transmitted radio signals 250 meters between different campus buildings in St. Petersburg.

23. The Russian Civil War (7 November 1917 – 25 October 1922) was sparked by the 1917 left-wing extremist October Revolution (see reference 14), as many parties vied to determine Russia's political future. It resulted in the formation of the Soviet Union.

24. The Russo-Japanese War (8 February 1904 – 5 September 1905) was fought between the Russian Empire and the Empire of Japan over rival imperial ambitions in Manchuria and the Korean Empire.

25. The Battle of Tsushima was the final naval battle of the Russo-Japanese War, fought on 27–28 May 1905 in the Tsushima Strait. It was a devastating defeat for the Imperial Russian Navy. More than 5,000 Russians were killed and 6,000 captured. The Japanese, which had lost no heavy ships, had 117 dead. The battle was the first in which wireless telegraphy played a critically important role.

26. Captain 2nd rank Nikolay Parfenovich Kurosh (1860–1907) was the flagship artilleryman of Rear Admiral Nebogatov (see reference 28) and sailed on the battleship Emperor Nikolay I (see reference 27), on which he was captured by the Japanese after the Battle of Tsushima (see reference 25). On 17 October 1907, trying to thwart the mutiny on the torpedo boat "Skory", he was killed by the left-wing extremist Jakov Poilov.

27. Imperator Nikolai I was a Russian battleship built for the Baltic Fleet in the late 1880s. She was slightly damaged during the Battle of Tsushima (see reference 25) and was surrendered, along with most of the Third Pacific Squadron, by Admiral Nebogatov to the Japanese.

28. Nikolai Ivanovich Nebogatov (1849–1922) was a rear admiral in the Imperial Russian Navy. On 28 May 1905, during the Battle of Tsushima, he surrendered five battleships under his command to the Japanese. Nebogatov was taken as a prisoner of war by the Japanese, and while a prisoner was dishonourably discharged by the Russian Admiralty and stripped of his titles of nobility. On his return to Russia, he and 77 of his subordinate officers were arrested and taken before a court martial in December 1906. Nebogatov's defense that his defective ships, guns and ammunition would have resulted in the meaningless slaughter of his men was rejected, and Nebogatov and three of his captains were sentenced to death by firing squad on 25 December 1906. However, the sentences were commuted to 10 years in prison by order of Emperor Nicholas II. Nebogatov was released from the prison in May 1909, when he was pardoned on the occasion of the emperor 's birthday. He moved to Moscow, where he died in 1922.

29. Baron Otto Theodor von Richter (1871 – missing in action 1920) was a Russian rear admiral who fought in the Battle of Tsushima. Pursued by the enemy, he beached his destroyer and blew it up, evacuating the crew to shore. The crew was later captured by a Japanese landing force. Richter participated in the suppression of unrest in the Baltics in 1905–1906.

30. The Semyonovsky Lifeguard Regiment was the second oldest guard regiment of the Imperial Russian Army, established by Peter the Great in 1691 at the village of Semyonovskoye (now in Moscow). The Preobrazhensky Regiment created in 1960 was the oldest. They distinguished themselves in battle during the wars with Sweden and the Ottoman Empire.

In 1905, the regiment played a key role in quelling the armed uprising in Moscow. On 16 December, when the Semyonovsky Regiment arrived in Moscow from Saint Petersburg, rebels still held some strategic important quarters of Moscow as well as the Moscow–Kazan Railway. Colonel Georgy Alexandrovich Min (1855–1906) and Colonel Nikolai Riman distinguished themselves in suppression of the mutiny. For these actions, Min received special praise from Emperor Nicholas II who promoted him to major general, and appointed to his personal entourage. Less than a year later, on 13 August 1906, General Min was assassinated by Zinaida Vasilievna Konoplyannikova (1878–1906) who was member of the Socialist Revolutionary Party.

31. Grand Duke Kirill Vladimirovich of Russia (1876–1938) was a grandson of Emperor Alexander II and a first cousin of Nicholas II, Russia's last emperor. He followed a career in the Imperial Russian Navy serving for 20 years in the Naval Guards. He took part in the Russo-Japanese War, barely surviving the sinking of the battleship Petropavlovsk at Port Arthur in April 1904. During the February Revolution of 1917, Kirill at the head of the Marine Guard, swore allegiance to the revolutionary Provisional Government, wearing a red band on his uniform. He also raised a red flag over his palace in Petrograd.

On 8 August 1924, Kirill declared himself "Guardian of the Throne" and on 31 August 1924 he assumed the title Emperor of all the Russians. By the laws of the Russian Empire, he was the legitimate heir to the throne. In 1929, Kirill became the undisputed leader of the monarchists. After claiming the throne, Kirill became known as the "Soviet Tsar" because in the event of a restoration of the monarchy, he intended to retain some of the features of the Soviet regime.

32. Louis Philippe II, Duke of Orléans (1747–1793), was a French Prince who supported the French Revolution. He was a cousin of King Louis XVI (1754–1793) and one of the wealthiest men in France. Due to the liberal ideology that separated Louis Philippe from the rest of his royal family, he always felt uncomfortable with his name and political connotations associated with it. As his name did not match with democratic and Enlightenment philosophy, Louis Philippe requested the Paris Commune allow his name to be changed, which was granted. He changed his surname to Égalité "equality". It was one of the three words in the motto of the French Revolution (Liberté, Égalité, Fraternité "Liberty, Equality, Fraternity").

33. The Battle of Galicia was waged between Russia and Austria-Hungary on 23 August – 11 September 1914. In the course of the battle, the Austro-Hungarian armies were severely defeated and forced out of Galicia; the Russians captured Lemberg (now Lviv) and ruled Eastern Galicia until their defeat at Gorlice and Tarnów (2 May – 13 July 1915).

34. Operation Albion (12 October – 20 October 1917) was a German air, land and naval operation in the First World War, against Russian forces with the aim to occupy the islands of Moonsund archipelago: Saaremaa (Ösel), Hiiumaa (Dagö) and Muhu (Moon). They were part of the Russian Empire and strategically dominated the central and northern Baltic Sea. The German army captured Hiiumaa (Dagö) on 13 October 1917. The Russian Baltic Fleet withdrew from the "Big Street" (German: Große Straße / Estonian: Suur väin) that separated Muhu from the Estonian mainland. The Germans claimed 20,000 prisoners and 100 guns captured during this operation.

35. The Stolypin agrarian reforms were a series of changes to Imperial Russia's agricultural sector instituted during the tenure of Prime Minister Pyotr Arkadyevich Stolypin (1862–1911). He was born in Dresden to a prominent Russian aristocratic family. In 1884, Stolypin married Olga von Neidhart, with whom he had five daughters and one son. He hoped to strengthen Russia by modernizing its rural economy. Modernity and efficiency, rather than democracy, were his goals. The reforms were aimed at transforming the traditional rural community form of Russian agriculture. The reforms began with the introduction of the unconditional right of individual landownership. They abolished the rural community system and replaced it with a capitalist-oriented private ownership. The reforms introduced development of large-scale individual farming, and agricultural cooperatives. They promoted agricultural education, and new methods of land improvement. The peasants received credits from the Peasants' Land Bank to purchase their own farms. Over 10 million persons migrated freely from western Russia to areas east of the Urals. This was encouraged by the Trans-Siberian Railroad Committee, which was personally headed by Tsar Nicholas II. The Stolypin agrarian reforms included resettlement benefits for peasants who moved to Siberia. On 1 September 1911, he was deadly wounded by Ukrainian Jewish lawyer Dmitrii Bogrov in Kyiv Opera House. Pyotr Arkadyevich Stolypin deceased on 5 September 1911.

36. Online unter: https://zeitpunkt.nrw/ulbms/periodical/zoom/21553870; das Original wird im Institut für Zeitungsforschung aufbewahrt.

37. Alexander Iwanowitsch Kuprin (*1870; † 1938) war ein russischer Schriftsteller. Er wurde als Sohn eines Beamten und einer tatarischen Adeligen in Narowtschat (Gouvernement Pensa) geboren. Inspiriert durch den Sieg Russlands im Russisch-Türkischen Krieg (1877–1878) wurde Kuprin 1880 an der Zweiten Moskauer Militärhochschule eingeschrieben und 1882 dem Kadettenkorps zugeteilt. Im Herbst 1888 verließ Kuprin das Kadettenkorps, um an die Alexander-Militärakademie in Moskau seine Fortbildung weiterzumachen. 1890 schloss er die Akademie als Leutnant ab und wurde zum 46. Dnjepr-Infanterieregiment in Proskurow (heute Chmelnyzkyj) versetzt, wo er die nächsten vier Jahre verbrachte. Während seiner Militärdienstzeit veröffentlichte Kuprin mehrere Kurzgeschichten, die schließlich zu seinem berühmtesten Werk „Das Duell" (1905) führten. Nach der Revolution von 1905 wurde Kuprin offen kritisch gegenüber dem Regime. Er knüpfte Kontakte zu Matrosen der Schwarzmeerflotte in Sewastopol und versuchte sogar, auf dem Schlachtschiff Potemkin anzuheuern, das im Juni 1905 meuterte. Als der Erste Weltkrieg ausbrach, eröffnete Kuprin in seinem Haus ein Militärkrankenhaus. Als Reserveoffizier wurde er im November 1914 einberufen und kommandierte bis Mai 1915 eine Infanteriekompanie in Finnland. Dann wurde er aus gesundheitlichen Gründen entlassen. Nach der Oktoberrevolution (7. November 1917) flüchtete Kuprin zunächst nach Finnland und wanderte schließlich 1920 nach Frankreich aus, wo er sich in Paris niederließ. In den Jahren in Paris erlebte Kuprin einen Rückgang seiner Kreativität und verfiel dem Alkoholismus. Ende 1936 entschloss er sich schließlich zur Ausreise nach Sowjetrussland. Die Jahre in Paris hatten seine Gesundheit ruiniert. Alexander Iwanowitsch Kuprin starb am 25. August 1938.

38. Eine Karikatur von Alexander Kuprins Erzählung „Das Duell" aus dem Jahr 1905:

Text oben: Moderner Don Quijote
Text unten: A. I. Kuprin mit seinem
Roman "DAS DUELL"
https://ruskontur.com/sharzh-1905-go-
da-na-povest-aleksandra-kuprina-poedinok

39. Wladimir Theodor von der Launitz (*1855; †1907) war Generalmajor, Gouverneur von Tambow (1902–1905) und ab dem 5. Januar 1906 bis zu seiner Ermordung (3. Januar 1907) – Bürgermeister von St. Petersburg. Während seiner Amtszeit als Bürgermeister nahm am 10. Mai 1906 die Staatsduma des Russischen Imperiums der 1. Einberufung ihre Arbeit auf, es wurden Kurse zur Ausbildung von Feuerwehrchefs organisiert, höhere Geschichts-, Literatur- und Rechtskurse für Frauen eröffnet usw. Während der revolutionären Ereignisse von 1905–1907 versuchte Launitz auf jede erdenkliche Weise, Terroristen entgegenzuwirken, und unterstützte offen monarchistische Organisationen wie die Union des russischen Volkes. Im Laufe einiger Jahre kam es zu 15 Attentaten auf sein Leben. Am 3. Januar 1907 wurde er während der Einweihung der Hauskirche der neuen Klinik für Haut- und Geschlechtskrankheiten des Kaiserlichen Instituts für experimentelle Medizin vom Terroristen Jewgeni Fjodorowitsch Kudrjawzew erschossen.

40. „Mir Boschi" (Gottes Welt) war eine literarische und populärwissenschaftliche Zeitschrift, die 1892 von Alexander Kuprins Schwiegermutter Alexandra Arkadjewna Dawydowa (*1849; †1902) gegründet wurde. Nach einer „politischen Bewertung" durch die Staatszensur wurde die Zeitschrift im Juli 1906 verboten und ihr Chefredakteur Fjodor Dmitrijewitsch Batjuschkow (*1857; †1920) vor Gericht gestellt. Allerdings erschien das Periodikum bereits ab Oktober 1906 unter dem neuen Titel „Sowremenny Mir" (Moderne Welt) wieder.

41. Die seit 1864 in Wien herausgegebene Zeitung „Neue Freie Presse" etablierte sich als führendes österreichisches Tageblatt, das insbesondere vom liberalen Bildungsbürgertum gelesen wurde. Karl Marx arbeitete zeitweise als Londoner Korrespondent dieser Gazette.

42. „Russkij Invalid" (Russischer Invalide) war die offizielle Zeitung des russischen Kriegsministeriums von 1813 bis 1917. Sie wurde von Paul Wilhelm von Pomian de Pesarovius (*1776; †1847) zu patriotischen und wohltätigen Zwecken gegründet. Die Einnahmen sollten behinderten Veteranen des Vaterländischen Krieges von 1812 sowie Soldatenwitwen und -waisen zugutekommen. Die erste Ausgabe der Zeitung, deren Herausgabe Alexander Pierre Paul Alexandre Joseph Pluchart (*1777; †1827) übernahm, erschien am 1. Februar 1813. Pesarovius füllte die Zeitung fast ausschließlich mit eigenen Artikeln. Bis zum Ende des ersten Monats hatte die Redaktion bereits 2.160 Rubel als Spenden erhalten. Sie veröffentlichte Nachrichten aus den Kriegsschauplätzen früher als andere Zeitungen, was dem „Russischen Invaliden" bei den Lesern großes Interesse bescherte.

Die Abonnements stiegen kontinuierlich. Große Spenden veranlassten Pesarovius 1813 zur Einrichtung eines unantastbaren Invaliditätskapitals, das ein Jahr später 395.000 Rubel betrug.

1814 übertrug Pesarovius dieses Kapital dem von Alexander I. gegründeten Komitee für die Verwundeten, zu dessen Mitglied er ernannt wurde. Während seiner Zeit als Herausgeber der Zeitung, die bis 1821 dauerte, überwies Pesarovius dem Komitee 1.032.424 Rubel. Seit 1830 wurde die Redaktion des „Russischen Invaliden" wieder Pesarovius übertragen, der diese Aufgaben bis zu seinem Tod wahrnahm. 1833 wurde Pesarovius zum Vizepräsidenten des St. Petersburger Evangelisch-Lutherischen General-Konsistoriums ernannt. Paul Wilhelm von Pomian de Pesarovius starb im Rang eines Geheimen Rates. Er wurde auf dem Lutherischen Smolenka Friedhof in St. Petersburg begraben.

43. Am 30. Oktober 1905 billigte Imperator Nikolaus II. die Schaffung **des ersten gesamtrussischen**

Parlaments – einer Staatsduma. Das Parlament war weitgehend von der Macht des Imperators abhängig. Die Duma wurde am 10. Mai 1906 von Nikolaus II. eröffnet, aber schon am 21. Juli 1906 aufgelöst. Der Grund dafür war, dass die Abgeordneten eine umfassende Agrarreform durchsetzen wollten, die der Imperator ablehnte. Die Proteste der Öffentlichkeit gegen die Auflösung der ersten Duma blieben unbeachtet. **Die zweite Staatsduma** tagte vom 20. Februar bis zum 2. Juni 1907. Die sozialistischen Parteien stellten im Parlament die Mehrheit. Die neuen Abgeordneten drangen noch kompromissloser auf die Lösung der Agrarfrage als ihre Vorgänger. Daher veranlasste Ministerpräsident Pjotr Stolypin den Imperator dazu, sie vorzeitig zu entlassen. Per Dekret vom 3. Juni 1907 änderte Nikolaus II. entgegen seinen Zusagen im Manifest vom 30. Oktober 1905 das Wahlrecht so ab, dass Städter, landlose Bauern und die nichtrussischen Minderheiten gegenüber dem russischen Großbürgertum und Adel stark benachteiligt wurden. **Die dritte Staatsduma**, die am 1. November 1907 zusammentrat, wurde von konservativen, nationalistischen und regierungstreuen Parteien dominiert. Dieses Parlament blieb die volle Legislaturperiode bis zum 9. Juni 1912 bestehen. **Die vierte Staatsduma** konstituierte sich am 15. November 1912. 1917 drängte die Duma-Mehrheit die letzte Regierung des Imperators zum Rücktritt und bildete aus sich heraus die Provisorische Regierung, welche die vierte Staatsduma am 6. Oktober 1917 auflöste.

44. Alexander Sergejewitsch Puschkin (*1799; † 1837) gilt als russischer Nationaldichter und Begründer der modernen russischen Literatur. Bis zum Großen Vaterländische Krieg 1812 sprach die russische Oberschicht Französisch. Puschkin schuf einen literarischen Stil, der untrennbar mit der russischen Literatur verbunden ist und zahlreiche russische Dichter sehr stark beeinflusste.

45. „Gott bewahre uns vor einem sinnlosen und gnadenlosen Aufstand in Russland. Diejenigen, die unmögliche Staatsstreiche bei uns planen, sind entweder jung und kennen unser Volk nicht, oder sie sind hartherzige Menschen, für die der Kopf eines anderen ein Pfennig und der eigene Hals eine Kopeke ist." (Alexander Sergejewitsch Puschkin: Die Hauptmannstochter).

46. Peter I., der Große (*1672; †1725), war von 1682 bis 1721 Zar und Großfürst von Russland und von 1721 bis zu seinem Ableben der erste Kaiser des Russischen Reichs. Energisch setzte er sich für die Förderung von Kultur, Bildung, und Wissenschaft in seinem Staat ein. Bei der Verwirklichung seiner Reformabsichten bediente sich der Zar vor allem der Deutschen Frühaufklärung, die in Russland im 18. Jahrhundert zur vorherrschenden Denkrichtung wurde. Die ersten bedeutenden russischen Wissenschaftler und Volksaufklärer wie z. B. Wassili Nikititsch Tatischtschew (*1686; †1750), Michail Wassiljewitsch Lomonossow (*1711; †1765) und Wassili Kirillowitsch Trediakowski (*1703; †1769) waren in höchstem Maße von deutschen Gelehrten wie Gottfried Wilhelm Leibniz (*1646; †1716) und Christian Wolff (*1679; †1754) beeinflusst.

Gottfried Wilhelm Leibniz
Kupferstich von Martin Bernigeroth
*(*1670; †1733)*
https://commons.wikimedia.org/wiki/

Christian Wolff
Kupferstich von Johann Georg Wille
*(*1715; †1808)*
https://commons.wikimedia.org/wiki/

Volodymyr Saviovskyi

Construction of a House in Polesia (Ukraine) in the 1950s
Зведення будинку на Поліссі (Україна) в 50-х роках минулого сторіччя

Prof. Dr. Volodymyr Saviovskyi
Technical University of Dortmund

Abstract

The article highlights the organizational and technological process for building houses in the rural areas of Ukraine in the 1950s. An example of construction of a cottage by folk craftsmen in one of the villages in Polesia is dwelled upon. Some features of the construction processes inherent in this region of Ukraine are indicated, with comments and comparisons pertaining to the current level of construction business. The composition of the organizational and preparatory stages of the construction of the house is also depicted. It is shown, how non-professional builders skillfully planned the process of building a house, procured building materials, selected the necessary equipment and devices. The terminology of the unique construction process is given in its original form – in the Polesian dialect of Ukraine. Some, almost forgotten constructing technical and technological procedures are shown based on empirical experience, reasonable expediency and ingenuity of masters of the past. It has been established that these technical solutions are currently scientifically substantiated as very appropriate and are in accordance with current building standards and regulations. This applies to such issues as engineering preparation of construction, working out of a structural design of the building with a supporting frame, thermal insulation of external enclosing structures, and the like. These age-old solutions have been finding their new revival in the modern technologies. The author describes a somewhat forgotten folk tradition of toloka – mutual aid. It is depicted not only as a process of erecting a house, but also as a social phenomenon. Toloka is a local, territorial community-wide undertaking to build a home for one particular family, or to construct other buildings or structures that serve individuals or the entire community. The whole village, men and women, old and young, gathered voluntarily. It was a kind of a festive working-together-event, similar to a ritual with some established rules and behavioral patterns. People gladly, free of charge, helped their neighbours. Toloka ended with a communal feast in the open-air dinner. Traditional national cuisine was prepared for participants. People ate, drank, joked and sincerely wished well the owners of the newly built house. The dinner went on till late at night. Folk songs could be heard in the whole borough. Generally speaking, toloka was a communal holiday of work and rest.

Some organizational and technical solutions of folk craftsmen of the past indicate ways to improve the existing ones and to develop new construction technologies. Since it can be asserted that "everything new is well-forgotten old."

Keywords: *organization and technology of construction | construction in the countryside | frame construction | insulation of buildings | toloka*
Ключові слова: *організація та технологія будівництва | будівництво на селі | каркасне будівництво | утеплення будівель | толока*

Досить часто в новітніх будівельних технологіях віднаходяться витоки давно забутих, давніх прийомів та підходів. Наприклад, широко відомий спосіб пересування важких кам'яних блоків, при будівництві єгипетських пірамід, в теперішні часи використовується для пересування цілих будівель та споруд. В 2017 році була збудована та згодом пересунута в проектне становище, найбільша споруда в світі – це нове укриття енергоблоку в Чорнобилі, масою 32,6 тисяч тон (!) [1, 2]. Інший приклад це установка 50-ти тонних мегалітів Стоунхенджу (Англія) в проектне положення, без вантажопідйомних механізмів. В теперішній час аналогічний прийом використовується, як ефективний «метод повороту» при установці опор ліній електропередачи та інших вертикальних конструкцій без допомоги будівельних кранів. Перелік таких прикладів можна продовжувати.

Багато технічних та технологічних рішень будівництва, котрі слугують прототипом новітніх розробок, можна віднайти й при розгляді будівництва звичайних будинків на селі в Україні. Одним з таких прикладів, котрий демонструє вище сказане, може слугувати опис зведення житлового будинку (хати) в селі Немиринці та Зелене Ружинського (тепер Бердичівського) району, Житомирської області. Село Немиринці стало відомим широкому загалу, дякуючи фольклорному фестивалю «Купальські роси» [3].

В подальшому, назви окремих будівельних процесів, терміни та вживані слова й окремі вирази, приводяться в автентичному звучанні, притаманному місцевому поліському діалекту.

При зведенні будь якого об'єкту, сучасна будівельна справа базується на попередньому обґрунтуванні його доцільності та розробці згодом проектної документації. Після узгодження проекту з замовником та підрядником, починається будівництво. А як же було в минулому, особливо в сільській місцевості? Формування та реалізація організаційно-технологічних рішень будівництва на селі можна продемонструвати на прикладі будівництва будинку (хати), котрий зводився в 50-х роках минулого століття. Народні будівничі ретельно планували майбутню будівлю. Місце розташування будинку, його конфігурація, кількість кімнат тощо, обдумувалось досить ґрунтовно, спираючись на наявні потреби, досвід минулих поколінь та народну мудрість. Ця мудрість передавалася в усній формі від покоління до покоління. Вона включає в себе багато цікавих та оригінальних рішень, котрі сьогодні можна кваліфікувати як підґрунтя новітніх технологій.

Однією з важливих сторін зведення будинку, була організації будівельних процесів, наявність та розподіл робочої сили. Цей аспект вирішувався унікальним явищем, характерним для тих часів, це будівництво будинку усією громадою, безкорисно. Це явище називалося толокою. ***Толока – це спільний для всієї місцевої, територіальної громади захід з будівництва будинку для однієї конкретної родини чи інших будівель та споруд, котрі потрібні для окремих осіб чи усієї громади. На толоку збиралось добровільно все село, чоловіки й жінки, старі й молоді. Це було свято спільної праці, свято допомоги один одному.***

В 50–60-ті роки минулого століття у вказаному вище регіоні України, люди будували будинки з дерев'яним несучим каркасом з влаштуванням самонесучих стін із глиняно-солом'яного розчину. Глиняно-солом'яні стіни носили лише огороджувальні функції. Дана конструкція розповсюджена широко і в інших регіонах України так і в Європі, наприклад фахверкові будинки в Німеччині [4]. Фундаменти виконували з місцевого каміння. Дахи – вальмові з покрівлею із соломи а пізніше з шиферу або покрівельної сталі.

Мрія про нову хату виношувалася в родині роками. Після того, як рішення було прийнято, вибране місце під майбутню хату, розпочинався підготовчий процес. Цей процес тягнувся кілька років. Він включав в себе усі його сучасні складові, а саме:

- організаційний період, що включав вибір місця будівництва, обдумування архітектурно-конструктивних та планувальних рішень будинку,

передбачувана послідовність процесів тощо;
- підготовчий період передбачав підготовку необхідних матеріально-технічних ресурсів (будівельні матеріали, конструкції, вироби тощо);
- технічний період, що передбачав придбання чи оренду транспорту, механізмів, інструменту, пристосувань (наприклад риштування, ящики для розчину, ємності для гашення вапна тощо);
- планово-економічний період передбачав розрахунок кошторису майбутніх витрат. В залежності від результатів розрахунку, та достатку родини, коригувалися усі вище наведені етапи.

По перше, потрібно було заготовити каміння для фундаменту. В селі Зеленому був невеличкий кар'єр з родовищем каміння – вапняку. Чоловіки кілька сезонів, за допомогою ручних інструментів, клинів та молотів, відколювали від масиву, окремі шматки каменю. Каміння підвозилися на *«підводах» (віз запряжений кіньми – прим. автора)* та складували на місці майбутньої будови. (Як було вказано вище, назви окремих будівельних процесів та окремі терміни наведено на місцевому діалекті). Також потрібно було заготовити пісок, купити цемент. Якщо на якомусь обійсті лежало каміння, пісок, то всі знали, що господарі готуються до будівництва. Наступним кроком потрібно було заготовити пиломатеріали на каркас будівлі, перекриття та дах. В селі це називали *«потрібно ліс заготовити»*. В майстра-столяра замовляли дерев'яні коробки чи рами дверних та віконних блоків. Їх називали *арцабами*. Далі потрібно було роздобути вогнетривку та звичайну цеглу для майбутньої печі та плити для приготування їжі та опалення. Плита опалення називалася в даному селі *«грубою»*. Одним з надважких питань було дістати, так тоді називався процес знайти та купити, покрівельний матеріал для даху – *шифер*. *(Шифер – азбестоцементні хвилясті листи – прим. автора)*. Часто за шифером приходилось їхати аж до Києва. Це основні матеріали. Також була ще ціла купа менш вагомих, але важливих матеріалів. Та про це згодом.

По мірі наявності на обійсті усіх, основних будівельних матеріалів, приступали до будівництва. Спочатку викопували траншеї під стрічкові фундаменти несучих стін майбутнього будинку. Траншею викопували глибиною близько 1,2–1,5 метрів. Копали до глибини де залягав міцний, щільний грунт. Ця глибина залягання фундаменту, як показує аналіз, відповідає сучасним будівельним нормам, як за несучою властивістю, так і коригується з вимогами сто-

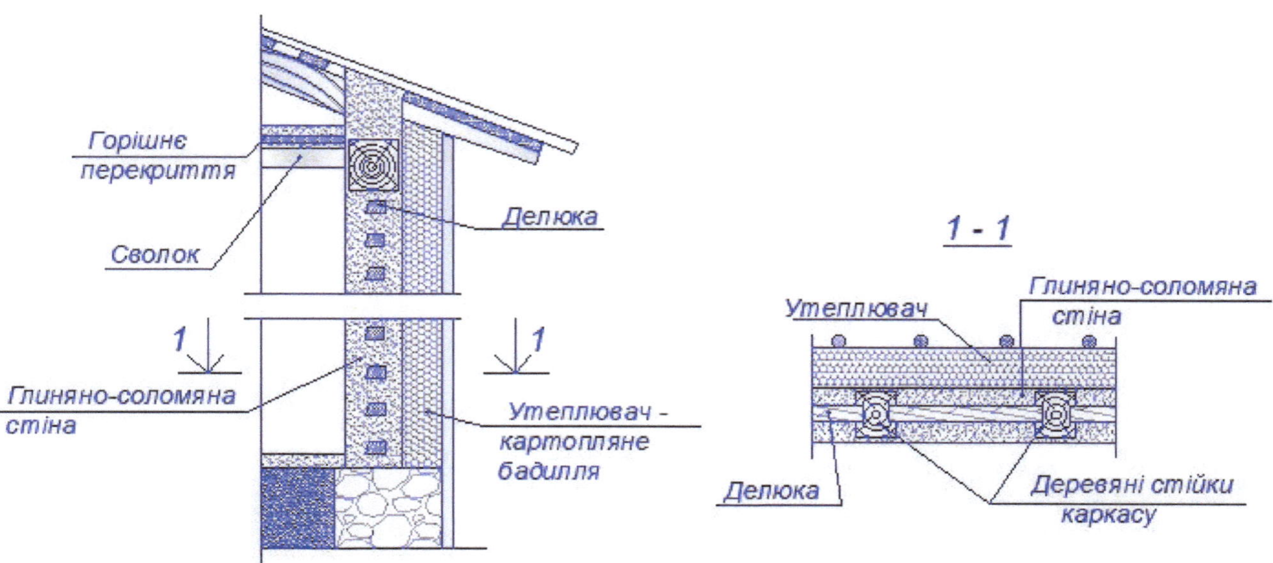

Рис. 1. Конструкція зовнішньої стіни будинку(хати) з тимчасовим утеплювачем

совно глибини промерзання ґрунту [5]. Готову траншею засипали дрібним камінням та заливали рідким цементно-піщаним розчином, тобто влаштовували монолітний бутобетонний фундамент. Інколи вкладали в конструкцію й металеві стрижні, чи що металеве «попадало під руку», тобто влаштовували залізобетонний фундамент. Надземну, цокольну частину фундаменту вимуровували з вапняку на цементно-вапняно-піщаному розчині. Називали цокольну частину фундаменту *«підмурком»*, а коли вже хата була готова, то ця частина називалася *«призьбою»* — місцем де можна було присісти для відпочинку. Фундаменти влаштовували для зовнішніх так і внутрішніх несучих стін. Зверху влаштованого фундаменту спочатку майстри зводили дерев'яні кроквяні конструкції даху. Це був мауерлат, крокви, лати та в'язі. Конструкції даху збирали тимчасово, нумерували і розбирали, складували поруч. Далі зводили весь каркас будинку. Для цього встановлювали та розкріплювали вертикальні дерев'яні стійки стін. Стійки встановлювали з кроком близько одного метра. В наведеному прикладу будівництва хати, для стійок використовували просмолені залізничні шпали. Була народна традиція класти під стійки, що розташовувалися в кутах будинку, дрібні монети, на щастя.

З бокових сторін вертикальних стійок влаштовували борозни (пази) на всю висоту чи до них прибивали напрямні рейки. В утворені пази встановлювали горизонтальні дерев'яні поперечини – *«делюки»*. Дані конструкції носили роль арматурного каркасу для послідуючого заповне-

ння огороджувальним матеріалом стін (рис.1). Делюки (фахверкові елементи) виготовлялись з грубо обробленого дерева – верби, що була місцевим недорогим будівельним матеріалом. Зверху стійок стін вкладали обв'язку (мауерлат) та несучі балки горішнього перекриття, які називали *«сволоками»*. Сволоки – це стругані з усіх боків балки з сосни, інколи з дубу. Так само простір між сволоками закладали делюками. Часто сволоки були відкритими на стелі в приміщенні. В цьому випадку глиняно-солом'яна накидка розташовувалась зверху них.

Зверху встановленого каркасу стін та несучих конструкцій горішнього перекриття збирали заздалегідь виготовлені, та складовані раніше поруч, конструкції кроквяного даху. Крокви також, були виготовлені з круглого лісу, як правило з сосни. Лати *(лати – дошки що з'єднували крокви та до них кріпили покрівельні матеріали – прим. автора)* виготовляли в вигляді необрізних дощок з верби. Дерев'яні брускові несучі елементи кріпилися один до одного спеціальними вузловими з'єднаннями та скобами. З'єднання кроквяних конструкцій типу «ластівчин хвіст», «в пів дерева», «паз-гребінь» чи інші потрібно було не тільки уміти виконати, але й знати їх механізм конструктивної роботи. Це зумовлювало необхідність знання хоча б основ будівельної механіки. Диву дається майстерність будівельників-самоучок. Знання та вміння будівельної справи передавалось здебільшого усно, від одного покоління до іншого. На рис.2 показаний процес зведення несучого каркасу будинку. Така конструктивна схема будинку являє собою яскравий приклад каркасного будівництва, котрий сьогодні являється провідним при зведені різноманітних будівель. В процесі роботи працівники робили короткі перерви для відпочинку та їжі. Місце для харчування облаштовували поруч (рис. 3). Обід тривав недовго.

ку чи вінок, котрий називається „*Richtkranz*" *(з нім. – святковий вінок – прим. автора).* Він обов'язково прибивається до дерев'яних конструкцій даху, або підвішується на гаку будівельного крану, якщо будівля з залізобетонним дахом (рис.4). Після зведення каркасу будинку влаштовувалось невелике свято.

Рис. 2. Зведення несучого каркасу та даху будинку в селі Немиринці (фото надано Б. Максименко)

Рис.4а. Гільце на даху дерев'яного даху

Рис. 3. Перерва на обід при зведенні каркасу будинку в селі Немиринці (фото надано Б. Максименко)

Рис.4б. Richtkranz (святковий вінок) в Німеччині

Про завершення зведення несучого каркасу та даху будинку свідчило прикріплення до конька *(самий верхній елемент даху – прим. автора)* гілки чи ялинки, прикрашеної квітами та кольоровими стрічками. Ця гілка називається «*гільце*». Гільце символізувало торжество та радість зведення будинку. Аналогічна традиція збереглась до нині у нас та за кордоном. Наприклад в Німеччині, також після зведення остову будівлі, на даху встановлюють прикрашену гіл-

Наступний будівельний процес – це заповнення каркасу стін та перекриття, тобто влаштування огороджувальних конструкцій стін та перекриття. В цей період в будівництві приймало участь все населення села й родичі з сусідніх сіл. Цей процес, взнаки значного обсягу робіт та високої трудомісткості, виконували **толокою**. До толоки також ретельно готувалися. Заповнення стін та перекриття виконували з глиняно-солом'яного розчину. Заготовляли глину, солому, інструменти, риштування тощо. Також проводилася й організаційна підготовка до забезпечення харчуванням робітників. В саду облаштовувалась просто неба імпровізована кухня, розставлялися довгі столи та лавки. Толока проводилася в вихідний день.

Наступав день толоки. На дорозі, поруч з будинком, що зводився, замішували глиняний розчин з соломою та водою. Солома слугувала армуючим компонентом, на кшталт сучасній фібрі. *(Фібра – металеві чи пластикові відрізки, що додаються до високоміцних бетонів, як армування – прим. автора).* Розчин змішували кіньми, котрі ходили колами по суміші глини, соломи та води. Далі готовий, густої консистенції, армований соломою розчин, чоловіки на носилках (ношах) підносили до місць укладки. Там з масиву розчину відділяли окремі невеликі об'єми, схожі за розміром на купу з кількох неформованих цеглин. Виділені частини розчину називали *«вальками»*. Вальки вкладали (*«накидали»*, *«мастили» стіни*) в стіни, заповнюючи простір між делюками дерев'яного каркасу (рис. 5, рис. 6). Вальки були тугими та пластичними й після укладки не розпливалися, а щільно облягали конструкції делюк. Розчин, після укладки в конструкцію достатньо швидко тужавів. По мірі зведення стін по висоті, встановлювали риштування. Так зводили зовнішні та внутрішні стіни та заповнювали (казали – *«накидали»*) горішнє перекриття. Жінки загладжували зовнішні поверхні глиняних стін долонями рук та дерев'яними гладилками, надаючи їм вертикальність та відносно гладеньку поверхню. Всі працювали голими руками.

Люди працювали намагаючись як найкраще виконати свою роботу. Ніяких розпорядників не було. За потреби люди кричали: «подавай сюди глину…» чи щось інше за потреби. Помічники негайно реагували. Робота супроводжувалась доброзичливими жартами та піднесенням від спільної праці.

Як вже згадувалось, важливим елементом толоки була організація відпочинку та харчування людей. Поруч, в саду готувався смачний обід. Люди сідали обідати за встановленими в саду довгими столами з лавками. Обід тривав не довго. Після обіду до пізнього вечора люди наполегливо працювали поки не добудували будинок.

Після того, як влаштування стін та горішнього перекриття було завершено, прибирали прилеглу територію від решток будівельних матеріалів, очищали інструменти та знаряддя.

Підліткам дозволялося їхати до ставу мити коней. Працівники приводили в порядок свою одежу, мили руки, й сідали за столи вечеряти.

Рис. 5. Толока. Заповнення каркасу стін глиняно-солом'яним розчином. Село Немиринці, 1957 рік. (фото надано Б. Максименко)

Рис. 6. Т Влаштування стін з глиняно-солом'яного розчину («мастили» стіни). Село Немиринці, 1957 рік. (фото надано Б. Максименко)

Про вечерю на толоці слід сказати окремо, стосовно традицій тієї пори. На вечерю завжди подавали традиційний суп «з вушками». *(Вушка – саморобні макаронні вироби схожі на маленькі раковини чи невеликі вушка (?) – прим. автора).* Вушка це особлива страва. Тісто для таких «макаронів» виготовляли самі господині. Воно розкочувалось тоненькими шарами та нарізувалося на невеличкі шматочки. Згодом, з цих шматочків, за допомогою веретена *(старовинний інструмент для прядіння – прим. автора)* виготовлялися вказані вироби (вушка) та висушувалися. Варився суп «з вушок» на концентрованому курячому бульйоні. З однієї миски черпали ложками одночасно кілька людей. Смачнішого супу майбуть немає в світі *(думка автора та багатьох, хто це куштував)*. Горохова чи гречана каша, котлети, обов'язково смажена риба, були голубці та різні овочі. На десерт був кисіль з вишень. Кисіль також їли разом кілька людей з однієї тарілки, своїми ложками. Хіба це не одна родина?

Дорослі випивали по чарці-другій самогонки, розмовляли, жартували. Проголошували тости за господарів та бажали їм щастя в новій хаті. Їй Богу, це було вкрай щиро. Це було добре, мирне свято, свято підтримки один одного, побажання добра. Дітей за столи тоді не садовили. Вони підходили до своїх матерів, а ті давали їм смачненьке зі столу: смажену рибу, голубці, котлети, пиріжки. Смачнішого нічого не було за вказані страви. Починало темніти, люди починали співати пісень. Заспівували (заводили) жінки та підхоплювали чоловіки. Вже давно стемніло, а люди співали й співали. ***Дякую вам односельчани за добрі спогади.*** Зведена хата ще стоїть і донині.

Завершення будівництва будинку потім ще тривало деякий час. По перше потрібно було, щоб глина стін та перекриття добре висохла. Потім потрібно було влаштувати перегородки, підлоги. Одним з важливіших елементів було будівництво печі з плитою. Зазвичай біля печі та плити влаштовувалась лежанка. Це найтепліше місце в хаті. Бувало, що діти спали на печі чи лежанці до повноліття, згодом їх заміняли літні люди. Останнім видом будівельних робіт була побілка стін та стелі хати. Для цього використовувалась біла глина, як фарбник. Вапняним розчином фарбували зовнішні поверхні стін. Призьба фарбувалася бітумним розчином.

Цікавим для фахівців може бути кілька конструктивних прийомів старих майстрів при будівництві. Наприклад для утеплення стін на зиму, влаштовували тимчасову теплоізоляцію. Для цього конструкція фундаменту, як було згадано вище, виступала десь 15–20 см за стіни. Дах також нависав десь на 40–50 сантиметрів. Так от, для утеплення стін вздовж фундаменту встановлювали вертикальні стійки з круглого дерева, кріплячи їх вверху до звису даху. Стійки встановлювали з кроком близько 50 сантиметрів. В утворений простір вкладали сухе бадилля з картоплі (рис. 1). Картопляне бадилля має трубчасту, порожнисту структуру, що придає йому високі теплозахисні властивості. Термічний опір теплопередачі шару з сухого бадилля товщиною близько 20 сантиметрів становить близько R=0,5 Вт/мК. Це відповідає захисним властивостям сучасного, ефективного утеплювача, на кшталт полістиролу, товщиною в 3–5 см. Чудове рішення, чи не так?.. Виробництво сучасних утеплювачів, якраз базується на створенні теплоізоляційних матеріалів з порожнистими структурами. Це мінераловатні, скловатні чи інші ніздрюваті утеплювачі. Так само й сучасна фасадна теплоізоляція типу «вентильований фасад» нагадує нам емпірично створене утеплення майстрами минулого [6]. Як видно будівельники й тоді чудово розумілися на будівельній теплофізиці.

Навесні, шар теплоізоляції з бадилля видалявся, а стійки розбиралися. Глиняна поверхня зовнішніх стін, за теплої пори року добре просушувалася.

Аналогічно використовувалось горище будинку. Літом воно заповнювалось соломою та сіном. Сухе збіжжя слугувало чудовим утеплювачем горішнього перекриття, й одночасно складом корму для скотини. Горище звільнялось від сіна вже пізньої весни з настанням тепла. Указані заходи чудово слугували забезпеченню комфортного температуро-вологісного стану в будинку.

Інший приклад кмітливості «старих» майстрів – це запобігання зволоженню підпілля. Часто підлоги в указані часи виконували глиняними *(глинобитними – прим. автора)*. Тобто глину для підлоги ущільнювали й зверху покривали рулонами з реліну чи різними килимками. В окремих оселях влаштовували дощаті підлоги. Щоб дошки та лаги підлоги не зволожувалися, та не пошкоджувалися біологічними шкідникам (грибками, комахами, жуками) їх потрібно було захищати. *(Лаги- балки-опори для кріплення дощок підлоги – прим. автора)*. Для цього використовували наступне рішення. На поверхню ґрунту підпілля насипали тоненький шар негашеного вапна. Також в стінках фундаменту влаштовували продухи (прорізи) для вентиляції підпілля. Так от, коли волога потрапляла в підпілля, вапно вступало з водою в хімічну реакцію, котра як відомо супроводжується виділенням тепла, яке підсушує простір. При потраплянні в підпілля якихось комах чи черв'яків, вони отримували «опіки» від вапна й покидали підпілля. Ось такий «хитрий» приклад мудрості «старих» будівельників.

Глиняні хати потрібно було кожного року підтримувати в належному стані, білити стіни, стелі, призьбу та інше. Пізніше в 70-роки минулого сторіччя глиняні будинки почали облицьовувати цеглою. Люди казали «обкласти хату цеглою». Так як фундамент мав виступ (призьбу), це дало змогу облицювати цеглою товщиною в «пів цеглини» *(пів цеглини – 12 см. – прим. автора)*. Між наявною стіною та додатковою цегляною, лицювальною верстою лишався повітряний прошарок, який став додатковим теплозахисним елементом. Після влаштування лицьового шару з цегли, підвищувались як захисні, декоративні так і теплоізоляційні властивості зовнішніх огороджувальних конструкцій стін. На рис.7 представлено вид такого будинку. Цей будинок справно слугує до сьогоднішнього дня.

Рис.7. Облицьована цегляною кладкою глиняна хата в селі Зелене. (фото В. Савйовський)

Наведений приклад будівництва житлових будинків на селі в 50–60 – ті роки минулого сторіччя вказує на вміння та знання простих людей, котрі спиралися на знання будівельної справи, отриманих багаторічним досвідом, розумною доцільністю та народною мудрістю. Також, згадана толока, як соціальне явище, являє собою приклад безкорисної взаємодопомоги для прийдешніх поколінь. З села, схожою дорогою (рис.8) в широкий світ, вийшло багато добрих людей, котрі понесли з собою вміння та досвід минулих поколінь.

Окремі організаційно-технологічні та технічні рішення народних майстрів минулого, стали підґрунтям сучасних методів будівництва та вказують на шляхи удосконалення наявних та розробку новітніх технологій в будівництві. Адже відомо: «що все нове – то давно забуте старе».

Рис. 8. Дорога з села, яка веде в широкий світ (Фото В. Савйовський)

Список літератури

1. Савйовський В.В. Реконструкція будівель та споруд. –К.: Вид. «Ліра-Л», 2017, 320 с.
2. Савйовський В.В., Молодід О.С. Зведення спеціальних будівель та споруд. Навчальний посібник. –К.: Видавництво «Ліра-К», 2018. – 248 с.
3. У Немиринцях грандіозно відзначили 15-й фестиваль «Купальскі роси». URL: https://www.zhitomir.info/news_176033.html(дата (дата звернення: 19.02.2024)
4. V. Saviovskyi. Instandsetzung von Gebäuden und Bauwerken. BoD-Books on Demand, Norderstedt, 2021
5. ДБН В.2.1-10:2018 Основи і фундаменти будівель та споруд. Основні положення. Мінрегіонбуд, 2018.
6. Савйовський В.В. Термомодернізація будівель: навчальний посібник – К.: Видавництво Ліра-К, 2021. – 242 с.

References

1. Saviovskyi V.V. Rekonstruktsiia budivel ta sporud. –K.: Vyd. «Lira-L», 2017, 320 s. {In Ukrainian}.
2. Saviovskyi V.V., Molodid O.S. Zvedennia spetsialnykh budivel ta sporud. Navchalnyi posibnyk. –K.: Vydavnytstvo «Lira-K», 2018. -248 s. {In Ukrainian}.
3. U Nemyryntsiakh hrandiozno vidznachyly 15-y festyval «Kupalski rosy». URL: https://www.zhitomir.info/news_176033.html. (data zvernennia: 19.02.2024). {Ukrainian}
4. V. Saviovskyi. Instandsetzung von Gebäuden und Bauwerken. BoD-Books on Demand, Norderstedt, 2021. {German}
5. DBN V.2.1-10:2018 Osnovy i fundamenty budivel ta sporud. Osnovni polozhennia. Minrehionbud, 2018. {Ukrainian}.
6. Saviovskyi V.V. Termomodernizatsiia budivel: navchalnyi posibnyk. - K.: Vydavnytstvo Lira-K, 2021. – 242 s. {Ukrainian}.

**K. J. Ibrayeva, Ileskan Smanov,
Gulnar Akhilbaeva, Asem Spabekova**

Scientific and Pedagogical Foundations of Teaching Eternal National Values

Мәңгілік Ел Құндылықтарын Оқытудың Ғылыми-Педагогикалық Негіздері

Ibrayeva, Kulyan Zhagiparovna
Doctor of Pedagogical Science, Professor
*Vocational Education Department of
S. Seifullin Kazakh Agro Technical Research
University,
Academician of Kazakhstan Academy of
Pedagogical Sciences,
Astana, Kazakhstan*

Smanov, Ileskan (Сманов, Илесхан)
Doctor of Pedagogical Sciences, Professor
*Department of Psychology
Faculty of History and Pedagogy
Zhanibekov South Kazakhstan Pedagogical
University, Shymkent, Republic of Kazakhstan*

Akhilbaeva Gulnar Islamkyzy, Ph.D.
*Zhanibekov South Kazakhstan Pedagogical
University, Shymkent, Republic of Kazakhstan*

Spabekova, Asem
Student, group 1101-12
*Zhanibekov South Kazakhstan Pedagogical
University, Shymkent, Republic of Kazakhstan*

Abstract

The modernisation of the education system in the Republic of Kazakhstan has become a state priority task. Its goal is the formation of a competitive human capital, introduction of the younger generation to the cultural values of the peoples of Kazakhstan based on the knowledge of the state language and history. One of the guiding documents is the educational standard resting on the Patriotic Act „Mangilik El“ developed and adopted on April 26, 2016, at the XXIV session of the Assembly of the People of Kazakhstan. It brings together different approaches to economic and political issues, morality and religion, and Kazakhstan‘s place in the globalised world. This document presents the unshakable pillars of the national idea of „Mangilik El“, which reflect the historical destiny and common interests of the people of Kazakhstan, as well as the guidelines for its development. In this regard, it is important to organize the educational process based on the values of „Mangilik El“, to introduce and implement its values in the pedagogical process. The celebration of the 550th anniversary of the Kazakh Khanate, which began with a solemn ceremony in Astana on September 11, 2015, was an important event in the history of Kazakhstani statehood. The authors are of the opinion that the roots of the achievements and successes of the multinational and multi-religious Kazakhstan lie in the good will, hospitality, and tolerance of its hard-working and peace-loving people who cherish traditional Kazakh values.

Keywords: *Kazakhstan | „Mangilik El“ | ethnopedagogy | educational process | patriotic education | integration*

Тірек сөздер: *патриоттық тәрбие, этникалық білім беру, тұлғаның дамуы, атнропологияялық бағыт, тарихи педагогикалық зерттеулер, құндылық.*

Бүгінгі таңда Қазақстан Республикасында білім беру жүйесі жаңғыртылуда. Отандық білім беруді жетілдіру қажеттілігі басым мемлекеттік міндеттер қатарына шықты: әлемдік дамыған 30 елдердің қатарына кіру үшін бәсекеге қабілетті адамзат капиталын қалыптастыру, өскелең ұрпақтың Қазақстан халықтарының ұлттық мәдени құндылықтары, мемлекеттік тіл, мемлекет тарихын білуге негізделген этномәдени және азаматтық бірегейлікті қалыптастыру бойынша әдістер және инновациялық технологиялар, тиімді механизмдерді енгізу, ашық азаматтық қоғам және әлемдік нарықтық экономиканың қажеттіліктеріне сәйкес өскелең ұрпаққа тәрбие және білім берудің сапасы мен деңгейін көтеруде, тәрбиеленушілердің патриоттық құндылықтарын қалыптастыру бойынша қазақстандық патриотизм идеясында тәрбиенің ұлттық жүйесін байытуда шетелдік тәжірибелерді қолдану. Зерттеу тақырыбымызға тікелей қатысты мәселе ретінде қарастырар болсақ «Мәңгілік Ел» идеясының құндылықтарын оқу үдерісінде басшылыққа алынатын кәсіби-құндылықты бағдар әдістемесін қолдауда оқу-тәрбие процесінде алатын орны ерекше. Өйткені, қоғамдық дамудың барлық негізгі кезеңдерімен, сол кезеңдердегі қоғамдық-саяси, әлеуметтік-экономикалық, мәдени қатынастармен, өзгерістермен, адамзат қоғамының тарихының барлық жақтарымен, қырларымен таныстырылатынын білеміз. Болашақ басшылыққа алынатын құжаттың бірі – кәсіби білім беру стандартында құзыреттіліктердің негізгі түрлері көрсетілген: Осы мақсатта 2016 жылғы 26 сәуірдегі Қазақстан халқы Ассамблеясының «Тәуелсіздік.

Келісім. Болашағы біртұтас ұлт» XXIV сессиясында «Мәңгілік Ел» патриоттық актісі әзірленіп, қабылданды. «Құндылық» «Отансүйгіштік» категориясының әдіснамалық, тарихи және педагогикалық қырларын ашып, атқаратын әлеуметтік қызметінің мазмұнын анықтап, жүйелеген зерттеулер қатарында философтар, мәдениеттанушылар А.У.Уразбеков, А.Ж.Тұрсынов, Г.Ж.Нұрышева, М.Вебер, Т.Х.Ғабитов , М.А.Дорохова, т.б. психологтар мен педагогтар С.Л.Рубинштейн, Қ.Б.Жарықбаев, К.Ж.Ибраева, Б.Гершунский, Т.Қ.Әтемова, Ә.Табылдиев, Т.С.Сламбекова, әлеуметтанушылар Н.Г.Лапин, С.Е.Нұрмұратов, т.б. атауға болады. [9]. Бұл зерттеулерде жасалған тұжырымдар зерттеу жұмысымыздағы ізденістерге бағдар болды. Отансүйгіштік тәрбие беру түркілік патриотизмнің көсемдері Тоныкөк, Томирис, Алып Ертоңға, Алып Манас (Алпамыс), Еділ батыр (Аттила), Едіге, Қобыланды батыр т.б. баһадүрлердің ісінен бастау алады және ұрпақ бойындағы ерлік сезімін оятып, туған жерге деген сүйіспеншілігін қалыптастыруда негізгі орынға ие.

Сонымен қатар, отансүйгіштік тәрбие беру мен атамекенге сүйіспеншілік туралы түркі ғұламаларының ой-пікірлері Күлтегін [2], Қорқыт Ата [3], Асан Қайғы [4], әл-Фараби [5], Ж.Баласағұн [6], М.Қашқари [7], Қ.А.Ясауи [8], т.б. мұраларында шешуші рөл атқарады.

Қазақстан Республикасының Президенті Н.Ә. Назарбаев «««Мәңгілік Ел» патриоттық актісі – бұл – қазақстандықтардың біртектілігі мен бірлігінің ауқымды да бірегей генетикалық бағдарламасы. Біздің рухани құндылықтарымыз бен ұмтылыстарымыздың негізгі форматын ұрпақтан ұрпаққа жеткізуі тиіс. Онда экономика мен саясаттың, мораль мен діннің мәселелері, Қазақстанның жаһандық әлемдегі орны жөніндегі көзқарастарымыз бір арнаға тоғыстырылған. Патриоттық акті біріншіден, халқымыз қалыптастырған және өз жан-жүйесінен өткерген басты жалпыұлттық құндылықтар, екіншіден, мемлекеттің, қоғамның және азаматтардың Қазақстанның тағдыры мен оны дамыту, өркендету жолындағы өзара жауапкершілігінің өзегі. Біз жаңа белестерге қарай ілгері басқан қадамымыздың дұрыстығын компаспен тексергендей, Патриоттық акт арқылы анықтайтын боламыз» – деді.

Құжатта Қазақстан халқының тарихи тағдыры мен жалпы мүдделері, біздің елімізді дамытудың базалық құндылықтары көрінетін «Мәңгілік Ел» жалпыұлттық идеясының жеті мызғымас тұғыры, жеті принциптері ұсынылған. Тәуелсіздік және Жалпыұлттық бірлік, бейбітшілік пен келісім, Зайырлы мемлекет және жоғары руханият, Инновация негізіндегі тұрақты экономикалық өсім, тарихтың, мәдениет пен тілдің ортақтығы, Ұлттық қауіпсіздік және Қазақстанның жалпы әлемдік және өңірлік проблемаларды шешуге жаһандық тұрғыдан қатысуы.

«Мәңгілік Ел» жалпыұлттық идеясы және басты құндылықтар толық нұсқада 2014 жылғы 14 қаңтардағы «Қазақстандық жол-2050: Бір мақсат, бір мүдде, бір болашақ» Елбасының халқына Жолдауында және 2014 жылғы 11 қарашадағы «Нұрлы жол – болашаққа бастар жол» Жолдауында айтылған болатын. Жаңа Қазақстандық Патриотизмнің идеялық негізі осы мемлекет құраушы ретінде жалпыұлттық құндылықтар мен тәуелсіздік жылдарындағы қазақстандық жол, қазақ халқының мыңжылдықтардағы тарихи тәжірибесін жүзеге асыру идеясын алға шығарды. Осыған орай; «Мәңгілік Ел» құндылықтары негізінде оқу-тәрбие үдерісін ұйымдастыру; құндылықтарды педагогикалық үдеріске енгізу және жүзеге асыру біздің мақсатымыз.

Белгіленген құндылықтарды жүзеге асыру Қазақстан Республикасының білім беру ұйымдарында «Мәңгілік Ел» патриоттық актісін түсіндіру бойынша жұмыстарды қамтиды.

Базалық құндылықтар негізінде тұлғаға тәрбие мен білім беру міндеттерін шешуде әлемдік және қазақстандық оңтайлы тәжірибелерге сүйенбеу мүмкін емес.

Патриотизм және патриоттық құндылықтар әлеуметтану, педагогика, саясаттану, тарих, философияда зерделеніп, тұжырымдамалық идеялар мен ғылыми тәсілдер тұрғысынан әртүрлі кезеңдер мен контекстерде ғалымдармен қарастырылады.

«Ұлы Дала елі», «Қазақ елі», «Мәңгілік ел» деген киелі ұғымдар талайлы тарихында басынан қилы қиындықты өткерген қазақ халқының бұрыны мен бүгінінен хабар беріп тұрғандай.

Елбасымыз тәуелсіздігімізді алғаннан бастап «Тұтас түркі елі» идеясынан «біртұтас Түркістан» идеясына дейінгі бабаларымыздың ізгі армандарын іске асыру ниетімен «Түркі бірлігі» идеясын айтып келеді. Көне түркілер аңсаған Мәңгілік Ел – бүгінгі қазақ мемлекеті. Ежелгі Ұлы даланың мұрагері, ұлтын сүйетін перзент,құнды дәстүрлердің мирасқоры ретінде қазақ елі басшысының «Мәңгілік Ел» идеясын жаңғыртуы – заңдылық әрі перзенттік парыз. Ұлт жасампаз болу үшін ұлтты ұйытатын ұлы идея қажеттілігін болмысымен сезінетін, мақсатсыз елдің тарих көшіне ілесуі неғайбыл екенін тереңнен пайымдайтын Елбасы Н.Ә.Назарбаев Қазақстан халқына кезекті жолдауында «Мәңгілік ел – ата-бабамыздың сан мың жылдан бергі асыл арманы екенін барлығымыз білеміз. Ол арман әлем елдерімен терезесі тең қатынас құратын, әлем картасынан ойып тұрып орын алатын тәуелсіз мемлекет атану еді. Ол арман тұрмысы бақуатты, түтіні түзу шыққан, ұрпағы ертеңіне сеніммен қарайтын бақытты ел болу еді. ...Ендігі ұрпақ – мәңгілік қазақтың перзенті. Ендеше, қазақ елінің ұлттық идеясы – Мәңгілік ел», – деп елді елең еткізген «Мәңгілік Ел» идеясын жариялады. Тарихқа тағзым жасап, бабалардың ұлы істерін ұлықтау – мемлекеттілік ұғымын ұлттық идеологияның алтын қазығына айналдыру. «Мемлекеттілік» ұғымы мемлекеттік құрылым ғана емес, мемлекеттілік – әр мемлекеттің дамуы мен қызметін ұйымдастыруға қажетті идеялар мен көзқарастардың тұтас жүйесі. Демек, «Мәңгілік Ел» идеясы – ұлттық-мемлекеттік идеяның іргетасы, елдің болашағына қызмет ететін жасампаз озық ой. Бір кездері дүркіреген Көктүріктер империясы ту етіп, Тоныкөк негізін қалаған, Мәңгі ел құндылығы бүгін, міне, осылайша Қазақстан мемлекетінің түп қазығы – ұлттық идеясына айналды. 2015 жылғы 11 қыркүйекте Астанадағы салтанатты жиыннан басталған Қазақ хандығының 550 жылдық мерейлі мерекесі ежелгі мемлекеттігімізді дүйім елге паш етті. Сәні мен мәні үйлескен торқалы той елдігіміз бен береке-бірлігіміздің, жарқын болашағымыз бен мәңгілік мұратымыздың бүкілхалықтық аламанына айналып, барша қазақстандықтарды, жалпы республика жұртшылығын бір серпілткені аян. Елбасының осы жиында: «Қазақ хандығы бұдан бес жарым ғасыр бұрын ғана шаңырақ көтерсе де, Еуразияның ұлы даласында орнаған арғы дәуірдегі сақ, ғұн, үйсін мемлекеттерінің, бергі замандағы Ұлы түрік қағандығы, Дешті Қыпшақ пен Алтын Орда мемлекеттерінің заңды мұрагері болды», – деп айтқан тұжырымы ондаған жылдар бойы қиянатқа ұшырап, көмескіленіп келген тарихи ақиқатқа шамшырақтай жарық шашып, тарихшы-ғалымдардың тиянақтайтын тұғырнамасына айналды.Халқымыздың береке-бірлігін паш етіп, мерейін тасытқан Қазақ хандығының 550 жылдық мерекесі қазан айында қасиетті Тараз төрінде үлкен табыспен, шарықтаған көңіл-күймен түйінделді. Алғаш рет «қазақ» атауымен ежелгі ордамыздың шаңырағы көтерілген көне Тараз жерінде мемлекет басшысының қатысуымен «Қазақ хандығы» монументі бой көтерді. Қазақ хандығының негізін қалаған айбынды хандар Керей мен Жәнібек қос қапталдағы тақта отырып, өздеріне ыстық ілтипат көрсетіп жатқан ұрпақтарын елдіктің мерекесімен құттықтап тұрғандай әсер қалдырады. Ән әуелетіп, шашулар шашқан халық көңілі – жаймашуақ.

Қазақ хандығының 550 жылдығы – тарихқа тағзым ғана емес, қазақтың жаңа сапаға көтерілуінің маңызды межесі, ұлт ұрпақтарына ой салып, отаншылдығын тереңдетудің, азаматтардың жүрегіне мемлекетшілдік сезімін ұялатудың жаңа бір мүмкіндігі болды. Көптің бірі болып тасада қалмай, дамыған, ықпалды мемлекет құруға ұмтылу – елдігімізге сын, ұлтымызды әлемге танытудың мүмкіндігі, қазіргі ұрпақтың асыл мұраты. Өйткені, әлемдік қатерлерге төтеп бере алатын қуатты мемлекет қана өміршең ел болатыны қазір ешкімге құпия емес. Ғажап ізденіс ғаламат жаңалық жасайтынын дәлелдеген Қазақстан Республикасының Президенті Н.Ә. Назарбаев «Қазақстан жолы – 2050: бір мақсат, бір мүдде, бір болашақ» Жолдауында қазақстандық жолдың келешекте қалай кемелденетінін, ең бастысы қандай ел құрумен тиянақталатынын түсіндіріп, жаңа дәуір келбетін сөзбен сомдап жеткізді. Әлемнің ең беделді жиыны – Біріккен Ұлттар Ұйымының мерейлі 70 жылдық сессиясында Елбасымыздың ана тілінде үн қатуы елді бір серпілткені аян. «Мәңгілік елдің»ұлттық тілі асқақтаса,ұлттың абыройы асқақтайтынын Ұлт көшбасшысы осылай дәлелдеді. Тіл – мемлекеттіліктің кепілі болса, елі мәңгі, ұлты мықты болатыны анық.

Рухы берік, арманы асқақ елдің азаматтары өзіне сенеді, өзгені сыйлайды,басқамен санасады, жақсысын үйренеді. Сондай азаматтар нағыз патриот болады, өз елін, жерін, Отанын сүйеді, халқының тілін, дәстүрін, мәдениетін, тарихын біледі, қадірлейді. Соны бағалап, үлгі алатындар көбейсе...«Мәңгілік ел» – Тәуелсіздік алғаннан кейін қалыптасқан, мыңжылдық мәні бар жалпыұлттық, философиялық идея. Көреген хандарымыз бен дана билеріміз, Алаш арыстары елін қайырымды қоғамға, қазақ жерін жайлы мекенге, Жерұйыққа айналдыруды арман етіп, сол үшін жанын да аямағаны тарихтан белгілі. Көпұлтты әрі көпдінді Қазақстанның алған асулары мен жеткен жетістіктерінің бастауы – бейбітсүйгіш халқымыздың ақ-адал пейілі мен қонақжайлылығы, төзімділігі мен еңбекқорлығы, елімізді мекендейтін түрлі ұлт өкілдерінің қазақтың дәстүрлі құндылықтарын қадірлеген дос пейілділігі. Сондай-ақ, жүз отызға жуық ұлттар мен он сегіз конфессиялық топ өкілдерінің береке-бірлігі жарасып, ынтымақтаса өмір сүруі – еліміздің бейбітшілік пен келісімді сақтау жолындағы ұтымды саясаты мен ауқымды еңбектерінің жемісі. Елбасымыз «Жер бетінде мыңдаған ұлттар мен ұлыстар бар. Біз – дербес мемлекет құру бақытына ие болған 193 ұлттың біріміз. Басқа бақыттың қонуы – бір бөлек, сол бақытты бағалай білу – бір бөлек... Тәуелсіздік – тарихтың сыйы немесе бүгінгі буынның меншігі емес. Ол – өткен бабалардың алдындағы қасиетті борыш және келешек ұрпақтың алдыңдағы зор жауапкершілік. Біз Тәуелсіздігімізге тәу етіп, тәубе деп, Тәуекелмен болашаққа бет түзеп келеміз. Біз бүгін Ұлы тарихымыздың тағы бір шебінен сенімді өтіп келеміз», – деген еді. Ата-бабамыздың сан ғасырлар бойы арманы, бүгінгі ұрпақтың ақиқаты болған қасиетті тәуелсіздігімізді, елдігімізді сақтап, дамыған елдердің қатарына қосылу – Мәңгілік ел болудың нысаны. Келешек ұрпақтың жарқын болашағы үшін әрқайсысымыз ортақ құндылыққа үлесімізді қосуымыз шарт. Бабалар арманы болған тәуелсіздікке қол жеткізген соң, оны сақтап қалу үшін ел ішіндегі алауыздыққа жол бермейтін біртұтас идея, алға жетелейтін бағыт-бағдар, мақсат-мұрат болу керек. Алдына асқақ мақсаттар қоятын, тілі мен дініне берік, жастары алғыр, рухы биік, жақсылыққа жаны құштар, ертеңіне сеніммен қарайтын халық қана тарихта «Мәңгілік ел» болып қалатыны анық. «Мәңгілік ел» идеясы – халықтың мүддесіне, қоғамдағы тыныштық пен ынтымақтастыққа қызмет ететін, бағыты мен бағдары анық жол, бейбітшілік пен келісімді, ұлтаралық татулық пен төзімділікті сақтап, сындарлы сәттерден сүріндірмейтін ұлы мұрат.

Бұрынғы-соңғы білімдарлардың пайымдауынша, елді ілгері сүйрейтін идея мемлекеттік сипат алып, қоғам мүшелерінің көңілінен шығуы үшін негізгі екі талап орындалуы тиіс екен.

Оның біріншісі – сол мемлекетте өмір сүріп отырған халықтың болмысымен, мақсат-мүддесімен толық сәйкес келуі;

Екіншісі – мемлекет тарихымен сабақтасып, ұзақ мерзімдер бойы сол қоғамда қалыпты, жетекші идеологиялық мәні болуы.

Ұлы қағанат құрған түркілер осы екі қағиданы да ұстанған екен.

Қазақ халқы Түркі қағандары мен Қазақ хандарының, Абай мен Алаш қайраткерлерінің ізгі арманы болған ұлттық идеологияны қалағандықтан, «Мәңгілік Ел» идеясын ту етіп көтеру қажеттілігін сезінді.

Қазақ елінің бүгінгі басты мақсаты – бірлігі жарасқан, экономикасы мығым, әлеуеті жоғары, бәсекелестікке қабілетті, алдыңғы қатарлы отыздыққа ену. Қазақтың біртуар перзенті Нұрсұлтан Әбішұлы тәуелсіздік алған күннен бастап құндылықтарымызды қадірлеп, асылымызды ардақтауға үндеп келеді. Бүкіл әлем қызыға қарайтын елдегі тыныштық пен тұрақтылық, экономикалық даму, ұлтаралық татулық – халқымыздың салқынқанды сабырлылығы мен Елбасымыздың сындарлы саясаткерлігінің жемісі.

Мемлекеттің тірегі – халықтар достығы, ел бірлігі, қоғам тұтастығы. Осы үш тұғыр бекем болса, Мәңгілік елдің шаңырағы биік, келешегі кемел.

«Мәңгілік ел» – кемел келешектің жобасы, сондықтан оның ұрпақтар сабақтастығына ұласатыны мәлім. Ұлы Дала елінің ғаламат тарихы мен қайталанбас құндылықтарын ұрпаққа ұлағаттап, үлгі болатындай игі істер атқару – бүгінге міндет, келешекке – аманат.

«Мәңгілік Ел» идеясын іске асыруды бастау бақыты бүгінгі ұрпаққа бұйырса, бабалардың алдындағы қарызымыз бен балалардың алдындағы парызымыздың орындалғаны. Қазақстан әлемдегі алып елдердің қатарынан өз орнын алса, әлемге танылған елдің өрендері ел мен жердің иесі болатындай намысты болып жетілсе, ұлттық дәстүрлі құндылықтарымыз жоғалмай, ұрпақтан-ұрпаққа беріліп отырса, «Мәңгілік ел» болашағы баянды, келешегі нұрлы болары айқын.

Қазақ хандығын құрған бабалар тағылымы, Ұлы Жеңіске жеткізген аталар ерлігі, елді біріктіруші күш – «Мәңгілік ел» идеясы жаңа Қазақстанды тың серпіліске бастап, арман ақиқатқа айналса, келешек ұрпақты ізгі ниеттерге жетелеп, отаншылдық рухын күшейте түсетіні анық.

Отаншылдық – елдікті, мемлекеттілікті саналы түрде сезіну, өз елінің бостандығы мен Тәуелсіздігін қорғау, Отанының тарихын құрметтеп, өзінің адал еңбегін туған елінің гүлденуіне арнау. Жастардың санасында шынайы патриоттық сезім мен Отанына деген адалдықты қалыптастыру – қазір бұрынғыдан да өткір, өзекті мәселе. Парасатты қоғам құру үшін жастардың бойындағы ұлтжандылығын шарықтату – әр біріміздің қасиетті парызымыз.

«Патриотизм – Отанға, мемлекетке деген сүйіспеншілік, жеке адамның аман-саулығы, өзінің мемлекетке тәуелді екенін мойындау, яғни патриотизм дегеніміз мемлекет деген ұғымды, оның жеке адаммен барлық жағынан өткені мен бүгінгі күні және болашағымен қарым-қатынасын білдіреді», – дейді қазақтың біртуар перзенті Б.Момышұлы.

«Қазақстандық патриотизмнің» ерекшелігі – тек қазақтардың ғана емес, кең-байтақ елімізді мекендейтін барлық ұлт пен ұлыс өкілдерінің тілегінің ортақ болуы, өзі мекендеп отырған елдің тағдырына алаңдап, жанашырлық жасауы. Отаншылдық – жерге деген іңкәрлік, халқының жетістігі мен еліңнің игілігіне қуана білу, ол – үздіксіз тәрбиенің нәтижесінде санада біртіндеп қалыптасатын ұлы сезім. Қазақстандық патриотизм өн бойына рух пен намысты жинақтаса, келешегіміз кемел, ұрпағымыз алғыр болары хақ.

Nur-Sultan
Nurai Talgat |

References / Әдебиеттер тізімі

1. ҚР Президенті – Елбасы Н.Ә.Назарбаевтың «Нұрлы Жол – Болашаққа Бастар Жол» атты Қазақстан халқына Жолдауы.2014 жыл 11 қараша. // http://www.akorda.kz/ (Address of the President of the Republic of Kazakhstan – Leader of the Nation N.A. Nazarbayev to the People of Kazakhstan "Nurly Zhol – A Path to the Future". November 11, 2014. // http://www.akorda.kz/).

2. Келімбетов Н. Ежелгі дәуір әдебиеті /Жоғары оқу орындарының филология факультеттері студенттеріне арналған оқулық. – Алматы: «Ана тілі», 1991. – 264 б. (Kelimbetov, N.: Ancient Literature / Textbook for students of philological faculties of higher educational institutions. "Ana tili", Almaty 1991; 264 р.).

3. Қорқыт Ата /Аударған Ә.Дербісәлин. – Алматы: «Қазақстан», 1993. – 108 б. (Korkyt Ata / Translated by A. Derbisalin. "Kazakhstan", Almaty 1993; 108 р.).

4. Қазақтың тәлімдік ой-пікір антологиясы / Құрастырған Қ.Жарықбаев, С.Қалиев. – Алматы: «Рауан», 1994. – 1-т. – 320 б. (Anthology of Kazakh Educational Thought, vol. 1 / Compiled by K. Zharykbayev, S. Kaliyev. "Rauan", Almaty 1994; 320 р.).

5. Әл-Фараби. Философиялық трактаттар. – Алматы, 1973. – 318 б. (Al-Farabi: Philosophical Treatises. Almaty 1973; 318 р.).

6. Баласағұн Ж. Құтты білік /Көне түркі тілінен аударған және алғысөзін, түсініктерін жазған А.Егеубаев. – Алматы: «Жазушы», 1986. – 616 б. (Balasagun, Zh.: Kutty Bilik / Translated from the Old Turkic language, preface and comments by A. Egeubayev. "Zhazushy", Almaty 1986; 616 р.).

7. Қашқари М. Түбі бір түркі тілі («Диуани лұғат ит-түрк»). – Алматы: «Ана тілі», 1993. – 192 б. (Kashkari, M.: The Original Turkic Language ["Diwani Dictionary of Turkic Languages"]. "Ana tili", Almaty 1993; 192 р.).

8. Ахметбек А. Қожа Ахмет Йассауи /Көмекші оқу құралы. – Алматы: «Санат», 1998. – 112 б. (Akhmetbek, A.: Khoja Akhmet Yassaui / Auxiliary textbook. "Sanat", Almaty 1998; 112 р.).

9. Ибраева К.Ж.: Этнопедагогика тюркоязычных мыслителей. Монография. 2009 г. Астана ТипКАТУ им. С.Сейфуллина 289с. (Ibraeva, K. Zh.: Ethnopedagogy of Turkic Thinkers / Monograph. S. Seifullin Kazakh Agro Technical Research University, Astana 2009; 289 р.)

Kazakh Folk Ornaments
Danagul Ospanbek

Walther Friesen

Villa Mengden in Sankt Petersburg
Villa Mengden in Saint Petersburg

Dr. Walther Friesen
Ausbildungs- und Forschungszentrum ETHNOS e.V.
Training and Research Center ETHNOS,
registered Association

Abstract
In September 2012, **the House of F. M. Sklyaev (Mansion of G. F. Mengden, Reserve House of the Winter Palace)**[1] was included in the Register of Cultural Heritage of St. Petersburg by order of the Russian Committee for State Control, Use and Protection of Historical and Cultural Monuments (KGIOP[2]).

In the 1710s, a two-story house was built on this site, belonging to a close confidant of the Russian Tsar Peter I (1672–1725),[3] bombardier[4] of the Preobrazhensky Life Guards Regiment[5] and ship-builder Feodosei Sklyaev (1672–1728). **Georg von Mengden** (1628–1703) was the first colonel and commander of this military unit for the personal protection of the Tsar. Service in this guard regiment was considered among officers a special privilege. All great and famous military leaders of the Russian Empire began their officer careers there. Sklyaev had no heirs, and after his death in 1728, the house became part of the state treasury.

In the 1730s, Empress Anna Ioannowna (1693–1740) donated the house and the property to the brother of the Russian regent Ernst Johann von Biron (1690–1772), Gustav von Biron (1695–1746).

In 1740, the "House of F. M. Sklyaev" was rebuilt for **Auguste Juliane von Mengden** (1719–1787). She was the first lady-in-waiting and friend of the Grand Duchess and Regent of the Russian Empire, Elisabeth Katharina Christine, Duchess of Mecklen-burg-Schwerin (1718–1746).

The ancestor of Auguste Juliane von Mengden was **Johann von Mengden, called Osthof** (†1469). From 1442 to 1450, he was Commander (Komtur) of Reval (now the Estonian capital Tallinn) and subsequently held the office of Land Master of the Teutonic Order in Livonia until 1469.

The rebuilt Mengden Villa (also called "Palace" and "Castle") was located between the Neva Embankment and the Great German Street (today: Millionnaya [Millionaires' Street]). It was the main street of the German Quarter – the architectural heart of Saint Petersburg.

In 1877, Lieutenant General of the Retinue of Emperor Alexander II (1818–1881), **Count Georg Theodor von Mengden** (Russian: Georgy Fedorovich Count Mengden; 1836–1902), acquired this palace, which was of great importance to descendants of the noble von Mengden family. Part of the Imperial Winter Palace actually became the "G. F. Mengden Mansion."

On October 22, 1878, **Zinaida Countess von Mengden** (1878–1950) was born in this mansion. Alexander II was the child's godfather; the godmother was Maria Feodorovna (née Marie Sophie Frederikke Dagmar, Princess of Denmark; 1847–1928), the wife of the future heir to the throne, Alexander III (1845–1894).

In March 1881, the Mengden Manor became the focus of police attention. Following the assassination of Russian Emperor Alexander II on March 1 (13), 1881, information emerged about an assassination attempt on the emperor that had been in preparation since the end of 1880. At the beginning of December 1880, the terrorists Anna Yakimova (1856–1942) and Yuri Bogdanovich (1849–1888) rented a cheese shop in the basement of the house under the name Kobozev. At the end of February 1881, a gallery was dug beneath the street, along which the emperor often passed, to store dynamite.

This event was discussed extensively in the press, and a short report on the subject also appeared in the "Dortmunder Zeitung" on March 17, 1881. This incident damaged the business reputation of Count Mengden, who, in the public's eyes, was indirectly involved in the assassination of the Russian emperor. In 1884, Count Mengden went bankrupt and lost most of his land holdings and the beautiful manor house.

His daughter Zinaida recalled: "Father innocently lost most of his fortune." The new Emperor Alexander III believed in the count's impeccable reputation, supported him in a difficult life situation, and provided the family with the opportunity to live in the Tauride Palace. The imperial family never ceased to care for the Mengden children.

Zinaida received an excellent education, possessed refined manners, and a direct, lively mind. Her godmother, Maria Feodorovna, mother of Nicholas II (1868–1918), drew attention to these qualities. She brought the girl closer to the court. In 1904, Countess Zinaida von Mengden was titled 'Dame d'honneur de la Ville' (Lady of Honor of the City of Saint Petersburg), and Empress Alexandra Feodorovna (née Princess Alix Viktoria Helene Luise Beatrix of Hesse and by Rhine), the wife of Emperor Nicholas II, appointed her to her court as a "gracious young lady."

During World War I, Zinaida assisted her godmother in establishing numerous hospitals and homes for homeless children. On behalf of the Empress, she participated in various charitable activities of the Russian Red Cross. When poison gases were used at the front, the Red Cross produced the breathing masks developed by scientist Nikolai Selinski (1861–1953), which saved many people's lives.

After the left-wing extremist coup in Russia in 1917, Zinaida followed her empress godmother to Denmark and settled in Hvidøre near Copenhagen. To earn a living, Zinaida Countess von Mengden opened a perfumery, which developed into a profitable business with a good reputation. She donated money to relatives remaining in Soviet Russia and to children in need.

From 1891 until his death, the imperial family's personal physician, **Nicolaus Theodor Zdekauer** (1815–1897), lived in the "G. F. Mengden Mansion." Zdekauer focused his fruitful work on issues of public hygiene. He did much to improve the sanitary situation in the capital of the Russian Empire. In 1878, Zdekauer opened the first meeting of the Russian Society for the Protection of Public Health, where he was elected permanent chairman; from that time on, he was the main initiator of its most important undertakings.

The Russian entrepreneur, statesman, finance minister and the first head of government of Russia **Sergei Yulievich Witte** (1849–1915), who belonged to the Baltic German knighthood of Pleskau,[6] also lived in this house for a certain period of time.

A fateful turning point in the use of the "G. F. Mengden Manor" is associated with the name of **Kamilla Trewer** (1892–1974). From 1902 to 1907, Trewer attended the German Petrischule, one of the most prestigious schools in St. Petersburg that Kamilla graduated with a gold medal. She then studied history and languages at the St. Petersburg Women's Pedagogical Institute. From 1913, Trewer worked at the Imperial Archaeological Commission, which was renamed the Russian Academy of History and Material Culture in 1919. That same year, she began her work at the Hermitage. In 1922, Trewer began to study the history and art of the Orient; at the same time, she attended lectures by Wilhelm Barthold (Russian: Vasily Bartold; 1869–1930), Joseph Orbeli (1887–1961), Sergei Oldenburg (1863–1934) and Alexander Freiman (1879–1968). In 1926, Trewer became a lecturer at the Department of Iranian Studies at Leningrad University and in 1928 she became Joseph Orbeli's assistant in the transformation of the Oriental Department of the Hermitage into an important scientific center for Oriental studies.

Over time, the "G. F. Mengden Mansion" was transformed into a research center dedicated to the interaction between Western and Oriental cultures. Currently, the house is part of the Hermitage State Art Museum. The Hermitage Scientific Complex is located here, with the state-of-the-art equipment that enables meticulous research into valuable paintings, sculptures, and works of decorative and applied art, as well as their restoration. The laboratory for the scientific restoration of oriental paintings is unique in the world.

On April 4, 2019, the State Hermitage Museum hosted the signing of a cooperation agreement between the State Hermitage Museum, Carl Zeiss Microscopy GmbH and the Russian Instrument-Making Company OPTEC (representative of Carl Zeiss in Russia). The tripartite agreement also included the creation of a joint scientific advisory center for participation in the international ZEISS Labs@Location program, which is being implemented by the Department of Scientific Restoration and Conservation of the State Hermitage Museum – i.e., in the "Mansion of G. F. Mengden." The agreement was signed by Mikhail Piotrovsky, Director General of the State Hermitage Museum; Nicholas von Korff, Managing Director of OPTEC GmbH; and Renata Burgemeister, Project Manager of Labs @ Location (Carl Zeiss Microscopy).

Today, the Mengden Mansion in Saint Petersburg is a platform and a clear example of the fruitful cooperation between Russia and Germany in understanding and preserving the world's cultural diversity.

***Keywords:** House of F. M. Sklyaev (Mansion of G. F. Mengden, Reserve House of the Winter Palace) | Georg von Mengden | Auguste Juliane von Mengden | Johann von Mengden, called Osthof | Count Georg Theodor von Mengden | Zinaida Countess von Mengden | Nicolaus Theodor Zdekauer | Sergei Witte | Kamilla Trewer*

***Stichwörter:** Haus von F. M. Sklyaev (Herrenhaus von G. F. Mengden, Reservehaus des Winterpalastes | Georg von Mengden | Auguste Juliane von Mengden | Johann von Mengden, genannt Osthof | Ernst von Mengden | Georg Theodor Graf von Mengden | Zinaida Gräfin von Mengden | Nicolaus Theodor Zdekauer | Sergei Witte | Kamilla Trewer*

Im September 2012, auf Anregung der Öffentlichkeit,[7] wurde das **„Haus von F. M. Sklyaev (Herrenhaus von G. F. Mengden, Reservehaus des Winterpalastes)",**[8] gemäß der Anordnung des Ausschusses für staatliche Kontrolle, Nutzung und Schutz historischer und kultureller Denkmäler (KGIOP[9]) in das Verzeichnis des Kulturerbes von St. Petersburg aufgenommen.

Das Schicksal bescherte diesem Haus eine abenteuerliche Geschichte voller Widersprüche. Heute spielt es als einzigartiges wissenschaftliches Zentrum der Eremitage – eines der größten und bedeutendsten Kunstmuseen der Welt – eine wichtige Rolle bei der Bewahrung des kulturellen Erbes der Menschheit und Stärkung der Völkerverständigung.

In den 1710er Jahren wurde an dieser Stelle ein zweistöckiges Haus errichtet, das einem engstem Vertrauten des russischen Zaren[10] Peter I. (*1672; †1725), Bombardieren[11] des Preobraschenski Leib-Garderegiments[12] und Schiffbauer Feodossei Sklyaev (*1672; †1728), gehörte. **Georg von Mengden** (*1628; †1703) war der erste Oberst und Kommandeur dieser Militäreinheit zum persönlichen Schutz des Zaren. Unter Offizieren galt es als ein besonderes Privileg, in diesem Garderegiment zu dienen. Alle großen und bekannten Heerführer des Russischen Imperiums hatten ihre Offizierslaufbahn dort begonnen. Sklyaev hatte keine Erben, und nach seinem Tod im Jahr 1728 ging das Haus in den Staatsschatz über.

In den 1730er Jahren schenkte Imperatorin Anna Ioannowna (*1693; †1740) das Haus mit dem Grundstück dem Bruder des russischen Regenten Ernst Johann von Biron (*1690; †1772), Gustav von Biron (*1695; †1746).

1740 baute der Schweizer Architekt Carlo Giuseppe Trezzini (*1697; †1768) das „Haus von F. M. Sklyaev" für **Auguste Juliane von Mengden** (*1719; †1787) um. Sie war die erste Hofdame und Freundin der Großfürstin und Regentin des Russischen Imperiums Elisabeth Katharina Christine Herzogin zu Mecklenburg-Schwerin (*1718; †1746). Der Vorfahr von Auguste Juliane von Mengden war **Johann von Mengden, genannt Osthof** (†1469). Von 1442 bis 1450 war er Komtur von Reval (heute – die estnische Hauptstadt Tallinn) und hatte danach bis 1469 das Amt des Landmeisters des Deutschen Ordens in Livland inne.

In der zweiten Hälfte des 16. Jahrhunderts schien es für viele ehemalige ostbaltische Mitglieder und Untertanen des Deutschen Ordens nur zwei Möglichkeiten zu geben: entweder sich irgendwie der drastisch geänderten geistlichen Umgebung anzupassen oder auszuwandern. Das Damoklesschwert der katholischen Rache hing weiterhin über den Köpfen der Lutheraner unter der polnischen Hoheit, die lutherischen Kirchenrituale durften in den schwedischen bzw. dänischen Besatzungszonen Livlands nur in den nationalen Sprachen der Besatzungsmächte ausgeübt werden.

*Der lutherische Glaube war im Zarentum Rus geduldet, und in vielen Aspekten konnten die Protestanten und die christlichen Andersgläubigen, wie z. B. die Anhänger der Lehre von Andreas Osiander (*1496; †1552), sich wesentlich sicherer in Ost- als in Westeuropa oder im Ostbaltikum fühlen. Der Militärdienst im Zarentum bot ihnen auch eine lukrative Perspektive. Den Offizieren und einfachen Kriegern wurde guter Sold aus dem Zarenschatz entrichtet. Für zuverlässige Dienste wurden ihnen Bodenanteile mit Leibeigenen in der fruchtbaren Schwarzerde-Zone Osteuropas, die vom Osmanischen Reich erobert worden war, zugeteilt.*

*Eine Gruppe von Deutschen aus Livland ließ sich in der Moskauer Vorstadt an den Ufern der Jausa, dem linken Nebenfluss der Moskwa, nieder. 1560 wurde dort die Lutherische Gemeinde gegründet, der der Sohn des friesischen Theologen Brictius thon Norde (*um 1490; †1557) vorstand. 1601 wurde auf Anordnung des Zaren Boris Fjodorowitsch Godunow (*1552; †1605) die lutherische Steinkirche in Moskau gebaut.*

*Zur gleichen Zeit erscheint auch **Ernst von Mengden (Großvater von Georg von Mengden)**, der zum anvertrauten hohen Hofamt von Stolnik aufstieg, und in dieser Rolle für die Verpflegung des Zaren verantwortlich war.*

Die umgebaute Villa Mengden (auch „Palast" und „Schloss" genannt) befand sich zwischen dem Newa-Fahrdamm und der Großen Deutschen Straße (heute: Millionnaja [Миллионная] „Die Straße der Millionäre"). Sie war die Hauptstraße des Deutschen Viertels – des Architekturkerns von Sankt Petersburg.

Der Palast grenzte unmittelbar an die kaiserliche Residenz, den Winterpalast, an.

*Karl Beggrov (*1799; †1875)*
Blick auf den Newa-Fahrdamm

Zu Beginn des 19. Jahrhunderts ging das Haus an Gräfin Irina Iwanowna Woronzowa (*1768; †1848) über, die den nächsten Umbau des Hauses und den Bau von steinernen Nebengebäuden im Hof initiierte. Die Woronzows besaßen das Haus etwa ein halbes Jahrhundert lang. 1860 kaufte das Kaiserliche Haushaltsministerium den Palast und es wurde Teil des Winterpalastes.

1877 erwarb Generalleutnant der Gefolge des Imperators Alexander II. (*1818; †1881), **Georg Theodor Graf von Mengden** (russ.: Georgy Fedorowitsch Graf Mengden; *1836; †1902), diesen Palast, der für Nachkommen des Adelsgeschlechts derer von Mengden von Bedeutung war. Sein Anwesen befand sich in Finnland, wo eine Fabrik zur Herstellung von Fensterglas betrieben wurde. Ein Teil des kaiserlichen Winterpalastes wurde tatsächlich zum „Herrenhaus von G. F. Mengden", was offiziell durch die oben erwähnte KGIOP-Anordnung bestätigt wird.

Von 1877 bis 1885 lebte dort Großfürst Alexej Alexandrowitsch (*1908; †1908), der vierte Sohn von Kaiser Alexander II. (*1818; †1881) und Kaiserin Maria Alexandrowna (née Maximiliane Wilhelmine Auguste Sophie Marie von Hessen und bei Rhein; *1824; †1880). Der Großfürst war Mitglied des Staatsrates, Chef der Flotte und der Seeabteilung sowie Vorsitzender des Admiralitätsrates.

Am 22. Oktober 1878 erblickte **Zinaida Gräfin von Mengden** (*1878; †1950) in diesem Herrenhaus das Licht der Welt. Alexander II. war der Taufpate des Kindes; die Taufpatin war Maria Fjodorowna (née Marie Sophie Frederikke Dagmar, Prinzessin von Dänemark; *1847; †1928), die Gemahlin des zukünftigen Thronfolgers Alexander III. (*1845; †1894).

Im März 1881 geriet das Mengden-Herrenhaus in den Mittelpunkt polizeilicher Aufmerksamkeit. Nach der Ermordung des russischen Imperators Alexander II. am 1. (13.) März 1881 tauchten Informationen über ein seit Ende 1880 vorbereitetes Attentat auf den Imperator auf. Schon Anfang Dezember 1880 mieteten die Terroristen Anna Yakimova (*1856; †1942) und Yuri Bogdanovich (*1849; †1888) unter dem Namen der Ehegatten Kobozev eine Käserei im Keller des Hauses. Ende Februar 1881 wurde unter der Straße, auf der der Kaiser oft vorbeikam, eine Galerie gegraben, um Dynamit zu verlegen.

Als die Arbeiten fast abgeschlossen waren, erregte Kobozevs Laden, der nur selten von Kunden besucht wurde, die Aufmerksamkeit des Hausmeisters eines Nachbarhauses, der die Polizei verständigte. Am 28. Februar, einen Tag vor dem Attentat, wurde das Geschäft im Beisein der Polizei unter dem Vorwand einer Hygienekontrolle inspiziert. Hinter der Holzvertäfelung war zu sehen, wie Erde aus dem Tunnel entnommen wurde. Auf dem Boden des Kellers waren deutliche Feuchtigkeitsflecken von frisch gegrabener Erde zu sehen. Kobozev-Bogdanovich erklärte, dass er die Räumlichkeiten renovierte und die Polizei deswegen keine Maßnahmen ergriff.

Dieses Ereignis wurde in der Presse ausführlich diskutiert. Und auch in „Dortmunder Zeitung" vom 17. März 1881 erschien ein kurzer Bericht zu diesem Thema:

Telegraphische Depesche
der „Dortmunder Zeitung".
* Petersburg, 17. März. An der Ecke des Newsky-Prospekt, in einer kleinen Gartenstraße wurde in einer im Hause Mengden, im Erdgeschoße gelegenen Käsebude am 16. März ein ausgegrabener Minengang entdeckt, der von dem Wohnzimmer des Inhabers der Bude ausgeht, die Oeffnung war unter einem Divan versteckt. Der Inhaber der Bude mit Frau flüchtete, Bude und Wohnung im Stich lassend. Der Divan ist mit Schutt ausgefüllt, eine Brechstange wurde vorgefunden. Die Mine war in der Richtung der kleinen Gartenstraße gegraben, welche zur Manege führt, gegenwärtig arbeitet eine Abteilung Pioniere an dem aufgefundenem Gange.

14

Dieser Vorfall beeinträchtigte den geschäftlichen Ruf von Graf Mengden, der in den Augen der Öffentlichkeit indirekt an der Ermordung des russischen Imperators beteiligt war. 1884 ging Graf Mengden bankrott und verlor den größten Teil seines Landbesitzes und das wunderschöne Herrenhaus. Seine Tochter Zinaida erinnerte sich: „Vater verlor unschuldig den größten Teil seines Vermögens." Der neue Imperator Alexander III. glaubte an den tadellosen Ruf des Grafen, unterstützte ihn in einer schwierigen Lebenssituation und verschaffte der Familie die Möglichkeit, im Taurischen Palais[15] zu wohnen. Die kaiserliche Familie hat nie aufgehört, sich um die Kinder der Familie Mengden zu kümmern.

Zinaida erhielt eine hervorragende Ausbildung, verfügte über raffinierte Manieren und einen direkten, lebhaften Geist. Ihre Taufpatin Maria Fjodorowna, Mutter von Nikolaus II. (1868; †1918), machte auf diese Eigenschaften aufmerksam. Sie brachte das Mädchen näher an den Hof. 1904 wurde Zinaida Gräfin von Mengden als 'Dame d'honneur de la Ville' (Ehrendame der Stadt Sankt Petersburg) tituliert und Imperatorin Alexandra Fjodorowna (née Prinzessin Alix Viktoria Helene Luise Beatrix von Hessen und bei Rhein), die Ehefrau vom Imperator Nikolaus II., bestellte sie zu ihrem Hofgefolge als „gnädiges Fräulein".

16

Am 19. Januar 1912 wurde Zinaida Gräfin von Mengden zur Hofdame erhoben und trat dem Gefolge der 1894 verwitweten Imperatorin Maria Fjodorowna bei. Während des 1. Weltkrieges unterstützte Zinaida ihre Taufpatin bei der Gründung zahlreicher Krankenhäuser und Heime für obdachlose Kinder. Im Auftrag der Imperatorin nahm sie an vielfältigen Wohltätigkeitsaktivitäten des Russischen Roten Kreuzes teil. Als an der Front Giftgase eingesetzt wurden, stellte das Rote Kreuz die von Wissenschaftler Nikolai Selinski (*1861; †1953) entwickelten Atemschutzmasken her, was vielen Menschen das Leben rettete. Nach dem linksextremistischen Umsturz von 1917 in Russland folgte Zinaida ihrer Imperatorin-Taufpatin nach Dänemark und sie ließen sich in Hvidøre bei Kopenhagen nieder. Um ihren Lebensunterhalt zu bestreiten, eröffnete Zinaida Gräfin von Mengden eine Parfümerie, die sich zum gewinnbringenden Unternehmen mit gutem Ruf entwickelte. Sie spendete Geld für die in Sowjetrussland verbliebenen Verwandten und für Kinder in Not.

Von 1891 bis zu seinem Ableben wohnte Leibarzt der kaiserlichen Familie **Nicolaus Theodor Zdekauer** (*1815; †1897) im „Herrenhaus von G. F. Mengden".

Karl Brüllow
Nicolaus Theodor Zdekauer

Zdekauer konzentrierte seine fruchtbare Arbeit auf Fragen der öffentlichen Hygiene. Er hat viel für Verbesserung der sanitären Lage in der Hauptstadt des Russischen Reiches getan. 1878 eröffnete Zdekauer die erste Versammlung der Russischen Gesellschaft zum Schutz der öffentlichen Gesundheit, bei der er von diesem Zeitpunkt an zum ständigen Vorsitzenden gewählt wurde und der Hauptinitiator ihrer wichtigsten Unternehmungen war.

Der russische Unternehmer, Staatsmann, Finanzminister und erster Regierungschef Russlands **Sergei Juljewitsch Witte** (*1849; †1915), der zur deutschbaltischen Ritterschaft von Pleskau[18] gehörte, wohnte für eine bestimmte Zeit auch in diesem Haus. Er setzte sich für eine Modernisierung des Russischen Imperiums ein, förderte eine stärkere Industrialisierung der Wirtschaft und forcierte den Bau der Transsibirischen Eisenbahn. Nach erniedrigender Niederlage Russlands auf dem Schlachtfeld im Russisch-Japanischen Krieg (1904–1905) wurde Witte im Juni 1905 als Chefunterhändler in die Vereinigten Staaten gesandt. Es hat ihm gelungen, relativ milde Vertragsbedingungen für Russland auszuhandeln.

Eine schicksalhafte Zäsur für die Nutzung des „Herrenhaus von G. F. Mengden" ist mit dem Namen von **Kamilla Trewer** (*1892; †1974) verbunden. 1902–1907 besuchte Trewer die deutsche Petrischule, die zu den prestigeträchtigsten Schulen in Sankt Petersburg gehörte. Kamilla schloss sie mit einer Goldmedaille ab. Anschließend studierte sie Geschichte und Sprachen am St. Petersburger Frauen-Pädagogik-Institut. Ab 1913 arbeitete Trewer in der Kaiserlichen Archäologischen Kommission, die 1919 in die Russische Akademie für Geschichte und materielle Kultur umbenannt wurde. Im selben Jahr begann sie ihre Arbeit in der Eremitage.

Junge Kamilla Trever

1922 begann Trewer sich mit der Geschichte und Kunst des Orients zu beschäftigen und hörte Vorlesungen von Wilhelm Barthold (russ.: Wassili Bartold; 1869; †1930), Joseph Orbeli (*1887; †1961), Sergei Oldenburg (*1863; †1934) und Alexander Freiman (*1879; †1968). 1926 wurde Trewer Dozentin am Lehrstuhl für Iranistik der Universität Leningrad und 1928 Assistentin Joseph Orbelis bei der Umwandlung der Orient-Abteilung der Eremitage in ein bedeutendes wissenschaftliches Zentrum der Orientalistik.

Mit der Zeit wandelte sich „Herrenhaus von G. F. Mengden" in ein Forschungszentrum, das sich mit der Interaktion der westlichen und orientalischen Kulturen befasste. Derzeit untersteht das Haus dem Staatlichen Kunstmuseum Eremitage. 1988 wurde es durch das Eremitage-Theater direkt mit den übrigen Eremitage-Gebäuden verbunden. 2017 wurde die Renovierung des „Herrenhauses von G. F. Mengden" abgeschlossen. Hier befindet sich der „Wissenschaftliche Komplex Eremitage" mit modernster Ausstattung, die eine akribische Erforschung von hochwertigen Gemälden, Skulpturen, Werken der dekorativen und angewandten Kunst sowie deren Restaurierung ermöglicht. Das Labor für die wissenschaftliche Restaurierung orientalischer Malerei ist einzigartig weltweit.

Am 4. April 2019 fand in der Staatlichen Eremitage die Unterzeichnung des Kooperationsvertrags zwischen der Staatlichen Eremitage, Carl Zeiss Microscopy GmbH und dem russischen Instrumentenbauunternehmen – OPTEC (Vertreter von Carl Zeiss in Russland) statt. Gegenstand der dreiseitigen Vereinbarung war auch die Schaffung eines gemeinsamen wissenschaftlichen Beratungszentrums für die Teilnahme am internationalen Programm ZEISS Labs@Location, das durch die Abteilung für wissenschaftliche Restaurierung und Konservierung der Staatlichen Eremitage – also im „Herrenhaus von G. F. Mengden" – umgesetzt wird. Die Vereinbarung wurde von Michail Piotrowski, Generaldirektor der Staatlichen Eremitage; Nicholas von Korff, Geschäftsführer der OPTEC GmbH und Renata Burgemeister, Projektleiterin Labs @ Location (Carl Zeiss Microscopy) unterzeichnet.

Heute ist das Herrenhaus derer von Mengden in Sankt Petersburg eine Plattform und ein klares Beispiel für die fruchtbare Zusammenarbeit zwischen Russland und Deutschland zum Verständnis und Erhalt der kulturellen Vielfalt der Welt.

References and Explanations / Referenzen und Erläuterungen

1. Dom F. M. Sklyayeva (osobnyak G. F. Mengdena, Zapasnoy dom Zimnego dvortsa)"
2. Komitet po gosudarstvennomu kontrolyu, ispol'zovaniyu i okhrane pamyatnikov istorii i kul'tury (KGIOP)
3. From 1721 until his death, Peter I was the first emperor (imperator) of the Russian Empire.
4. Bombardier (German: Bombardier) is a rank in the artillery, introduced in 1682 for the artillerymen of the so-called "amusing / toy army" of Peter I Alekseevich, the future Tsar/Emperor Peter the Great, who served in the bombardment company he founded with the rank of captain (company commander).

5. In 1691, Peter the Great's so-called "toy army" was divided into the Preobrazhensky Regiment and the Semyonovsky Regiment. The Preobrazhensky Regiment, along with the Semyonovsky Regiment, the Izmailovsky Life Guards Regiment, and the Life Guards Jaeger Regiment was considered the "Old Guard". These were the oldest regiments in the Russian Empire. Among officers, serving in one of these guard regiments was considered a special privilege. However, officer ranks were generally open only to the nobility.

6. Pleskau (Russian also Pskov) was the administrative center of the democratic Pskov Republic in north-western Russia (1200s–1510).

7. http://www.damals-im-osten.de/index.php/projekte/11-russlanddeutsche-geschichte/43-mengden-schlo esser-villas-und-palaeste

8. „Dom F. M. Sklyayeva (osobnyak G. F. Mengdena, Zapasnoy dom Zimnego dvortsa)"

9. Komitet po gosudarstvennomu kontrolyu, ispol'zovaniyu i okhrane pamyatnikov istorii i kul'tury (KGIOP).

10. Von 1721 bis zu seinem Tod war Peter I. der erste Kaiser (Imperator) des Russischen Imperiums.

11. Bombardier war ein Rang in der Artillerie, der 1682 für die Artilleristen der sogenannten „amüsanten / Spielzeugarmee" von Peter I. Alekseevich, dem zukünftigen Zaren/Imperator Peter dem Großen eingeführt wurde, die in der von ihm gegründeten Bombardierungskompanie dienten. Er selbst hatte den Rang eines Hauptmanns (Kompanieführers) inne.

12. 1691 wurde das sogenannte „Spielzeugarmee" Peters des Großen in das Preobraschenski-Regiment und das Semjonowski-Regiment aufgeteilt. Das Preobraschenski-Regiment galt daher neben dem Semjonowski-Regiment, dem Ismailowski Leibgarde-Regiment und dem Leibgarde-Jägerregiment auch als „Alte Garde". Diese waren die ältesten Regimenter des Russischen Imperiums. Unter Offizieren galt es als ein besonderes Privileg, in einem von diesen Garderegimentern zu dienen. Allerdings standen die Offiziersränge meist nur dem Adel offen.

13. https://commons.wikimedia.org/wiki/File:Beggrov2.jpg?uselang=fr

14. Beitrag in der Dortmunder Zeitung Nr. 75 vom 17. März 1881; online unter: https://zeitpunkt.nrw/ulbms/periodical/zoom/1352151; Original im Institut für Zeitungsforschung.

15. Das Taurische Palais (Taurisches Schloss) wurde 1789 vom russischen Architekten Iwan Jegorowitsch Starow (*1745; †1808) fertiggestellt. Imperator Paul I. (*1754; †1801) erwarb das Bauwerk und gestaltete es zur Kaserne für das Gardekavallerieregiment um.

Alexander I. (*1777; †1825) ließ es wieder als Residenz restaurieren.

16. https://ruskline.ru/analitika/2008/07/26/vospominaniya_grafini_zinaidy_georgievny_mengden_1878–1950_frejliny_imperatricy_marii_fedorovny

17. https://commons.wikimedia.org/wiki/File:Брюллов_Портрет_Н._Ф._Здекауэра.jpg

18. Pleskau (russisch auch Pskow) war das Verwaltungszentrum der demokratischen Republik Pskow im Nordwesten Russlands (1200er–1510).

19. https://commons.wikimedia.org/wiki/File:Kamilla_Trever.jpg

Herrenhaus von G. F. Mengden,
Reservehaus des Winterpalastes
Autor: "A.Savin, Wikipedia"

Erhaltene Grundmauern
von Haus Mengede in Dortmund-Mengede
Fotografin: Tatiana Friesen

Hugo Wormsbecher

Russia-Germans:
Special National Policy – Forever?

Hugo (Gustavovich) Wormsbecher was born in 1938 in the Autonomous Soviet Socialist Republic of the Volga Germans. In 1941, he was exiled to Siberia, where he grew up. He worked as a turner, electrician, in a topographical expedition in the semi-deserts of Kazakhstan and in the Alatau Mountains, as a teacher, then – as a staff of the editorial boards of the newspapers "Freundschaft" (Friendship) in Zelinograd (today Nur-Sultan) and "Neues Leben" (New Life) in Moskau. He was the author of several books, novels, short stories, screenplays and numerous publications on history, culture, literature, current problems of the Russia-Germans. Hugo Wormsbecher had been a member of the USSR's Association of Journalists since 1969 and a member of the Writers' Association of the USSR since 1988. He had been in the midst of the movement of the Russia-Germans for their rehabilitation since 1963. Hugo Wormsbecher participated in the first two Russia-German delegations to Moscow in 1965. Since 1989, he had been fully integrated into the movement of the Russia-Germans: he was one of the founders of the society 'Wiedergeburt' (Rebirth), of the International Association of the Russia-Germans, and of the Federal Cultural Autonomy of the Russia-Germans. Hugo Wormsbecher died on 20 November 2024 in Moscow.

Abstract

In one of his last articles Hugo Wormsbecher contemplates on the destiny of Germans in Russia. He is of the opinion that Russia for many years has lacked a national policy, the goals and objectives of its leadership are unclear and incomprehensible in this respect. The Germans in the Tsarist Russia made their contribution to the formation, development and defence of the great country. After the Decree of 28 August 1941, they had to struggle to survive as a people striving to obtain equal rights with other ethnic groups of the multinational USSR. For many years the Russia-Germans have been deprived not only of equal rights with other nations of the country and of its own national home, but also of national life. Deprived even of the opportunity to live together, and thus of the opportunity to work for themselves, to solve their own national needs with their own efforts. They have been also deprived of the opportunity to fully reveal their well-known industrious mentality. And to realize themselves fully – in the interests of the country. In 1991, the Law "On the Rehabilitation of Repressed Peoples" was adopted, the Russian-German Protocol on Cooperation in Restoring the Statehood of Russian Germans (1992) was signed, and an Intergovernmental Commission for its implementation was created. But their statehood was substituted by "cultural events" donated by Germany. Hugo Wormsbecher suggests that Russia-Germans could be accommodated in one of the "advanced development territories" designed and financed by the Russian government. And the results of this nationally-oriented project could be further developed and adapted to the conditions of other regions.

Keywords: Hugo Wormsbecher | Russia-Germans | Soviet Germans | autonomous German republic | advanced development territories

1. Three Sisters from Different Fathers:
Humanity and Its National Policies

In an infinitely multinational world, the national question has apparently always played a major role, which is becoming even more and more important today. And we can note three main approaches to it that have developed over the centuries.

The first strategy (in America and increasingly in Europe) implies that nationality, like religion, is "separated from the state" and it is a personal matter. The entire population is considered a "nation". However, the concepts of population, nation, nationality, people – rarely coincide in any country. Even in a society of unbridled consumption, where the main interests of the individual and the masses are switched over to satisfying constantly evolving consumer demands, such a method of reducing the significance of the national question is, for the time being, quite effective. Especially at the stage of the semi-starved existence of the masses: after all, first of all, everyone thinks not about preserving their national peculiarities, but about survival in general. This approach, among others, has one significant drawback: the development of consumerism constantly develops demands and requires their timely satisfaction, otherwise the ideas that have taken hold of the masses at a subsistence minimum can also actualize the national question (remember the collapse of the USSR) that they are apt to turn into a revolutionary force capable of sweeping away everything.

The second approach, more typical for fairly mono-national states of the Far, Near and Middle

East, evolves under a highly raised national flag. When religion-ideology is not separated from the state, but on the contrary, the state is subordinated to it. When people are faithful to traditions and strictly regulate life according to them. When freedoms of society and of an individual are very dependent on the historical and cultural development of the country itself. When the education of society and of an individual is carried out in the spirit of respect for their own way of life and rejection of the expansion of someone else's lifestyle. This ensures, if necessary, maximum mobilization of the people for paramount challenges that are perceived simultaneously as both national and religious-ideological. "Other" national issues, if they do appear in such countries, are simply neglected by the masses of the titular nation.

The third pathway, uniquely developed in the super-multinational pre-revolutionary Russia[1] and then thoroughly consolidated in the USSR, is to preserve the areas of residence of the annexed or voluntarily joined peoples, their national-territorial formations, their languages, cultures, and ways of life that have evolved over the centuries. The commonwealth state provided them not only with the protection from external threats, but also guaranteed equality with other peoples of the country: national self-government, representation in government bodies, development of national education and culture, and satisfaction of other national demands. The introduction of the common state language opened up opportunities for them to fully participate in the economic, political, cultural and social life of the country and for the broad self-realization of individuals and associated nations. This attitude to "national question" led gradually – and without conflicts! – to the formation in each associated nation and every person of an ever-greater potential for common knowledge, culture, education, common interests, values, common features in the national character and – to an ever greater and non-violent formation of a "common civil identity" without infringing on national identity, i.e. to the formation of an increasingly united commonwealth nation.

2. National Policy in Today's Russia: In a Coma, in Intensive Care or at a Crossroads?

Over the past 30 years, Russia has once again in its history found itself faced with the need to solve three main problems: to survive as a state, to ensure its security and to revive its economy. And it has solved them – quite convincingly. However, it is strange: the authorities, while intriguing their own people and the whole world, maintain a clandestine silence about their ultimate goal. And in national politics, it seems, they have strictly classified their current goals, tasks, and state of affairs. Even during the annual direct lines with the president over all the years, among hundreds (or already thousands?) of questions voiced out of millions asked from all over the country, not even once (!) any "national" question has been asked.

So, everyone could only guess whether the national policy in Russia causes everyone to be inexpressibly delighted, completely depriving them of the power of speech. Or whether this is just a peculiarity of standard electronic communication rules, as with the prohibition of usage of obscene words on the Internet. Or maybe this national policy is in a deep coma. Or it has been transferred to intensive care. Or it, like a knight at a crossroads, has thought hard in front of a slanted signpost of new directions. Let's not guess, which path it will choose. Let's take a closer look at the situation...

***

For many years now, Russia has lacked a national policy that would be consistent with its high, state significance in such a multinational country; its goals and objectives are unclear and incomprehensible, and the introduction of market "self-sufficiency" is increasingly reducing it to the level of contract amateurism in all its spheres.

In the *"scientific sphere"*, its interests and level are largely determined by those who are the purchasers of the research, and, naturally, to what extent the opinions of the employers are more important to the salaried specialists themselves than the future of their country.

In the *area of management*, it does not have a clear program of action, the necessary funding, and its next all-round special managers, temporarily responsible for the "situation", are mainly busy inventing and searching for arguments and "facts" for positive reports to the "top".

In the *sphere of implementation* of such permitted projects, one can sometimes observe once-living ideas and "encouraged" salaried enthusiasts who process facts and data pertaining not only to the local level. But in the end, it usually turns out to be just the dried fruit of the popular TV show "Play, accordion!":[2] ethnically coloured costumes, dances, melodies – that happens, but "where is the state national policy" – that's a big question. Because *such an accordion* plays only for complete assimilation, and only the one who orders such music hears it. National policy, the task and essence of which should be the timely (or better yet, proactive) satisfaction of the national demands of all the peoples of the country and at all levels through trustful cooperation between the peoples and the state and thereby ensuring sustainable interethnic peace, is replaced at the managerial level by supervisory and control measures with the by authorities beloved predictable-plastic monitoring confirming anything.

At the *executive level*, a super-urgent task is the formation of a "civil identity" instead of a national identity, which is perceived by the authorities as an obvious relic of the past. And for the *general public* – episodically nationally coloured amateur shows "From Moscow to the borders."[3] All this is especially clearly manifested in the special national policy "for Russia-Germans" in the absence of any other forms of "concern for the people" ...

3. "The Question of Russia-Germans": Their Mummification Instead of Rehabilitation?

It is precisely the third pathway from those mentioned above that Russia-Germans could have successfully followed, like everyone else. But they did not.

Their completely different fate was determined by two important circumstances inherent only to them: firstly, the very extraordinary role destined for them in the history of Russia; and secondly, their very "un-Russian" nationality with a mentality formed outside of Russia. After all, they were invited to Russia to help it solve the most serious problems facing the country, so they went through the strictest "casting", which inevitably and for a long time distinguished them in the new environment even more than in the environment from which they were chosen, and determined the widest range of attitudes towards them at different levels, including over time the most negative ones. And their nationality, during critical periods in the country's history, became a grave crime, and they have not been rehabilitated to this day.

The Germans in the Tsarist Russia made the expected contribution to the formation, development and defence of the great country, which has no analogue to this day; also (and mainly) at the administrative level.

After the revolution[4] and the civil war,[5] their role was politically, socially and class-wise firmly relegated to the "agrarian sector". *During the Great Patriotic War,*[6] the sphere of their relations with their homeland, Russia, was already fenced off with barbed wire, as was their still unmarked, nameless labour contribution to the common Victory – a contribution to work in the rear, but with a mortality rate

higher than at the front. And *after the war*, barbed wire with guards was replaced, apparently, by a more profitable regime of special settlements and special commandant's offices for survivors and those being born, with 20 years of hard labour for violating it, and with a guaranteed eternal "everything is under control" regarding the Russia-German's nationality.

The Russia-Germans, starting with the Decree of August 28, 1941, had to accomplish another incredible feat – the feat of national survival. To do it as a sacred duty to the departed fathers, to their children with silent incomprehension in their wide-open eyes, and to their future descendants – so that they could remain in the history of their country, in the memory of its peoples, and in history in general, not endlessly slandered by their own country, but as who they really were: its worthy people, who had not tarnished themselves in any way, despite everything.

And they accomplished this feat as a deeply internal protest of each person against all the accusations, repressions, discriminations and injustices that this Decree has brought down on four generations of Russia-Germans just because of their nationality, and they continue to do it to this day...

This was the case until the collapse of the USSR. True, before its tragic decline, the Law "On the Rehabilitation of Repressed Peoples" (1991) was adopted, the "Russian-German Protocol on Cooperation in Restoring the Statehood of Russia-Germans" (1992) was signed, and an Intergovernmental Commission for its implementation was created. However, then again "something went wrong."

4. Instead of Statehood – Amateur Performances with German Aid?

The latest major event in this "something went wrong" is the decree of President V. Putin (January 2016) on amendments to the decree of the former Russian president Boris Yeltsin (1992) with removing from it the words about the restoration of the statehood of Russia-Germans. Another decree, which caused a new heartbreaking pain in the people, who had already seen and experienced so much injustice from various decrees, which was soon intensified by another meeting of the Intergovernmental Commission (May 2016), where not a word was said about the rehabilitation of Russia-Germans...

I have already had to note that, in general, this decree is difficult to reconcile with the President's well-known attentive attitude towards any people and towards the national question in general. But since there have been no amendments to this decree, no "moratorium" on its implementation, or even an official explanatory commentary on it, it is quite understandable that in the minds of those whose long-standing hopes this decree has once again so traumatically destroyed, it is associated entirely with Putin who signed it.

Although it would be more logical to perceive it as yet another result of the long-standing anti-autonomist campaign in the Volga region[7] and its support by some influential figures in the President's "close circle", who do not miss an opportunity to discredit President, especially in such seemingly "purely technical" but in fact a very resonant issue for him…

But decrees are not issued for guess-who-contemplations; so, the very fact of its appearance can hardly be considered just as someone's private machinations. Well, everything that followed looked like just a tactic for implementing the decree: and the "updating" of the Russian-German Protocol through its complete emasculation, which was done by the FADN[8] (Federal Agency for Ethnic Affairs). The new liquidation goals had to be given the appearance of at least some justification and support from the "masses". To this end, they tried to pass off the previous goals of the national movement of Russia-Germans, as well as the laws and decisions adopted on them, including the still officially valid "Russian-German Protocol on Cooperation in Restoring the Statehood of Russia-Germans", as simply "outdated" and having lost their significance. For this purpose, they habitually used the old "arguments" of these again so selectively heard "masses".

"Opinions" have increasingly begun to be expressed, including in the "publications of Russia-Germans", that these same Russia-Germans as a people have never existed, do not exist, and cannot exist; that the majority of those who still considered themselves Germans have long since "returned to their historical homeland", that is, to Germany; that only an "insignificant minority" remains in Russia and these have already lost all of their German identity or are no longer interested in it at all. And those who left for Germany will "never again" return to stepmother Russia. And from all this, naturally, it follows that there is no one left to implement the "Law On the Rehabilitation of Repressed Peoples" and the corresponding Russian-German Protocol.

And so, the only thing that is still "really needed" today for the Germans who still remain in Russia is at least some, at least sometimes, "cultural events", so that no one suddenly thinks that no one here knows anything about them and does not want to know, and does not come again to the idea of this anti-decree rehabilitation. And that this cultural program should be carried out, naturally, at Germany's expense: after all, it itself has long since committed itself to helping soften the consequences of the war for the Russia-Germans who suffered so much from it! (Which again causes an ambiguous attitude towards "these Germans": were they the only ones in the country who suffered from this war? Why should Germany help only… them?).

But the main thing is that the execution of this important international cultural program can only be entrusted to one authority: someone who has long mastered the unique and highly sought-after profession of "working as a German" and has invaluable experience in providing the necessary funeral services in this area.

Of course, it was not easy to implement all this, but with the support of the giants of the new national policy to replace the national identity of the peoples with a civil identity in the great multinational country, success was inevitable. Another question: is this success really in the interests of the country? To get at least some idea of this, let's take a short excursion into recent history...

5. What Kind of "Unity" is Required to Restore Justice? And Who is Interested in It?

The national movement of Russia-Germans for rehabilitation arose more than 60 years ago and reached the peak of its mass character and support among the people by the beginning of the 1990s. It was united by a single big goal – to achieve the restoration of the illegally seized statehood, and great hopes that this goal was close. At its core, the movement was courageously constructive and, despite the tragic history of its people, was able to avoid unwanted excesses, establish serious relationships with the authorities and achieve the adoption of all necessary decisions, even at the international level.

However, gradually, in the course of the increasingly unbridled "democratization" of the country, when the government increasingly lost the ability to implement the decisions it had made, the people's trust in the government and their belief that with such a government their goal could be achieved weakened rapidly. And because of that the credibility of the constructive forces in the movement diminished increasingly, populist radicalism became more and more active, and through this the unity of the movement was to a great extent destroyed.

This process reached its limit after B. Yeltsin's speech in the Saratov region (08.01.1992), where the "guarantor of the Constitution" at a mass rally specially assembled for him declared to the whole world that "there will be no German autonomy!" He mockingly suggested that instead of restoring their republic, „these Germans could settle at the Kapustin Yar military training ground",[9] dig up the unexploded shells there, with which "the earth is filled", and "let Germany help." The response was a mass exodus of almost 2.5 million people.

After such a collapse of both a common goal and unifying hopes, the German movement has already split devastatingly into two directions: one – in favour of continuing to strive for rehabilitation, despite everything ("Yeltsins come and go, but without rehabilitation we have no future").

Another movement, much more widespread and now having gained trump cards that justify any radicalism, is for the immediate departure of everyone to Germany, "so that at least our children remain Germans."

With the issue of rehabilitation completely got frozen for the time unpredictable, the first direction also found itself facing a very difficult problem: how to preserve the German identity, native language, and national culture of Russia-Germans who remained, despite everything, in Russia? Save it when the people have not had a single national school for 50 years? And for 50 years the people have been scattered across vast territories? And for 50 years they have not had their own governing bodies and sources of support? And there isn't any sign of that now? In such a situation, every public organization of Russia-Germans – federal, regional, and local – had to survive on its own now. Moreover, in the conditions of "shock therapy" and a bandit "market" in an increasingly destroyed country. Thus, a systemic fragmentation of the movement occurred, and it found itself in a tough dilemma: to stop all its efforts altogether or to find at least some sources of support to continue these efforts.

It is needless to say that in this situation, the aid provided by Germany to Russia to support its Germans was practically the only "source". And therefore, the determining one? But both sides of the Intergovernmental Commission participated in its distribution, that is, both German and Russian officials. And it turned out that now the obligatory condition for receiving this aid was no longer participation in cooperation on the restoration of statehood, but... the rejection of the idea of restoring statehood, which for some reason the aid distributors on both sides were now categorically against.

The courageous attempts of the national movement to preserve at least in some form its structures, still advocating for rehabilitation, and first of all the federal ones (Federal National-Cultural Autonomy "Russia-Germans" – FNKA RN,[10] Gemeinschaft e.V. usw.), without state support from Russia and without help from Germany. If they were now successful to some extent, then only with the personal funds of several of their leaders, for which they later paid dearly. But their names will forever be inscribed in the history of the movement.

However, soon a raider takeover of the FNKA RN by the private family undertaking "International Union of German Culture" – MSNK[11] was prepared and carried out, then an illegitimate "new FNKA congress" was held, where an illegitimate "new FNKA leadership" was elected. And finally, with the open forgery of legal documents and with the direct support of the "administrative resource", a "new FNKA" was registered – from among those who were bought with the financing of "projects" or whose hands were simply forced. Two Moscow courts found this "registration" illegal, but their decisions were overturned, which speaks to the level of "administrative resources" involved…

But about half of the regional NKAs still ***did not join*** this "new FNKA". They created the Association of Non-Aligned NKAs (mainly in Siberia, where the majority of Germans in Russia still live), which, naturally, was now completely ignored by both Russian and German officials.

Thus, the once united German movement suffered its biggest "split" that had been long-controlled from outside. It is clear that such "lack of unity" will disappear as soon as the state again has the goal of rehabilitating the people or when at least the conditions for financing "projects" (that even exclude thoughts of rehabilitating the people) change.

In the meantime, officials from both sides are habitually shedding crocodile tears over the "lack" of the unity that Russia-Germans "need". At the same time, however, no one has ever explained what kind of exceptional unity Russia-Germans must have so that they, like other repressed peoples, could finally receive the right to rehabilitation, to the restoration of their statehood, to a national future? And who, and in what way, should make up this unity? Should it be all Russia-Germans, without exception, who were forcibly dispersed 80 years ago, and who have been living in this dispersion during all these years, with vigilant prevention of their compact residence? Or should "at least" the Germans of several today sovereign countries – Russia, Kazakhstan, Kyrgyzstan, Ukraine, and with them several million already living in Germany be united? Or are only the Germans of today's Russia enough? But they too must first "live all together"?

And if so, then: who and how should allow them, not to mention provide, such cohabitation? And where? Or should they provide it for themselves? And is such "unity" of precisely all Germans in Russia obligatory? And if not all, then how many? And can anything else be considered unity other than living together? For example, the same desire to have a future as a people, that is, to have, like all other repressed peoples, their own statehood, for which Russian Germans have been fighting for all these 80 years?

And who will determine and check the availability of any of these necessary unities? Will the highest authority be some officials of another "specialized" department with their updated sly monitoring? Or will the decisive word in this matter continue to be held, as it has been the case for many years by carefully selected "working Germans", in whose special-cultural-structures, endlessly parasitizing on the tragedy of the people, everything is done to replace its national identity with a "civil identity" as quickly as possible. And where it is forbidden to even remember such seditious words as rehabilitation, restoration of justice, statehood? Or will the scientific proof of the absence of such unity continue to be the profound conclusions of the well-salaried special scientists that Russia-Germans no longer need any kind of statehood, and that even talking about it is harmful? Or will the opinion of those still living Russia-Germans who have gone through the entire tragic history of their people, through endless repressions, discrimination, injustice and deception, and have lost faith in the possibility of waiting for any justice in this world so much that they bitterly reject even any hint of it, be recognized as equally convincing?..

But perhaps there is a much simpler way to restore justice and equality for Russia-Germans? For example, for the government itself to at least briefly discover the ordeal they have gone through. If it would feel out the repressions and discriminations that had been unknown to it for so long, which every single one of the Russia-Germans had gone through. It would discover their long-standing hopes, which have not been justified to this day – under any leader neither of the USSR nor the Russian Federation! – for justice to come to them too. It would discover the scale, tenacity, courage, and endurance of their national movement in the most difficult conditions for 60 years. It would discover their united, as never before, rejection of the most mocking refusal to restore their statehood by the "guarantor of the Constitution". It would discover for a moment and feel – at least for this moment of enlightenment! – what the entire people felt and still feel.

The Russian government would discover at least the purely economic damage to the country from the departure of 2.5 million "good workers and law-abiding citizens" – more than 100 billion dollars (this is only at the time of departure; and what has it become over the past 30 years?). And the demographic damage to the country from this departure. And the damage from the loss of its educated (mostly Russian-speaking!), cultural, moral, ethical potential, which has been created for so long and with such difficulty and has been suddenly lost by Russia, is also of no small importance for the country...

6. Or Maybe We Should Remember about "Territories of Advanced Development"?..

For 80 years, an entire nation – several million people! – has been seeking to restore its equality in its country. 60 years ago, the country itself recognized as false all the accusations levelled at this people because of its nationality. 30 years ago, the country itself decided to restore its illegally liquidated statehood. But… it has not been able to implement this decision to this day.

Yes, there were other, even larger and more serious questions – questions of the very survival of the country. But today many of them have already been resolved, and thoroughly! When will the question of restoring justice to its last unrehabilitated people be resolved? The Russia-Germans have not been rehabilitated only because they worked too well for their country? And when the country, which by the utmost exertion of strength and willpower of those who always remember their filial duty to it, has once again been raised from ruins to one of the world's leading powers, will finally voice the answer to this question? The answer that an entire nation has been seeking for 80 years?! When?

Doesn't anyone in this government feel sorrow any more for their great multinational state? For a state that was once truly united by the friendship of its peoples, which allowed it to withstand the enormous test of the Great Patriotic War? Does Russia still remember its great past? Including the significance of its unique experience in the national question? Its centuries-old experience of ensuring peaceful coexistence in one country of hundreds of peoples, nationalities and tribes of different levels of historical development, different cultures, religions, different ways of life, and traditions? Does it also comprehend the unique two-century experience of tsarist Russia, which, in the absence of its own necessary personnel, strategically wisely called the Germans into its service from outside in order to make a historic breakthrough with their help: in the development of the country, in the development of its statehood, economy, military affairs, in the development of science, culture, art, education, in the development of its own territories and natural resources?

And perhaps, it is also reflecting on the 80-year experience of its special national policy in relation to only one of its peoples? And such a bitter result for the country? Is it reflecting on and... preparing an answer to the long-standing question of this people: is such a special national policy really determined for it, and only for it, – forever? Or will its statehood be restored, as it was long ago restored for its other peoples? And possibly restored using some updated methods and tempo for that?

For example, remembering such a project as the creation of "advanced development territories". In order to thoroughly work it out as a large-scale and comprehensively beneficial venture for the country. And maybe design it with a clear national accent: for whom and why.

So that the people, who have been deprived of their national home in their own country for so many years, could also find it again. And with it, find faith in their national future, which they themselves, despite everything, consider possible only in Russia.

For so many years the Russia-Germans have been deprived not only of equal rights with other nations of the country and of its own national home, but also of national life. Deprived even of the opportunity to live together, and thus of the opportunity to work for themselves, to solve their own national needs with their own efforts. They have been also deprived of the opportunity to fully reveal their well-known industrious mentality. And to realize themselves fully – in the interests of the country.

And if we also take into account all the potential that the people have (there are more than 10 million Russia-Germans and their descendants in the world on different continents who still remember well what a great country they come from!), then it goes without saying what the creation of such an "advanced development territory" could give instead of the present-day stalemate national policy! And what significance could such a decision have for the multinational Russia! New economic, scientific, educational, social projects could be developed and adapted to the conditions of other regions! And needless to say, what a resonance such a decision could cause in other countries, among other peoples. With their ever-growing interest in Russia in general and in its experience and heritage specifically in the sphere of national politics.

(2021, October)

Comments and References

1. The October Revolution was a state coup staged by left-extremists in Russia in 1917. It began through an insurrection in Petrograd (now Saint Petersburg) on 7 November 1917.

2. "Play, accordion!" is a Soviet and Russian television program dedicated to Russian folk music in Russia. The program has been broadcast since 1986 on Channel One and airs on Sundays.

3. "Wide Is My Motherland" is a Soviet patriotic song from 1936. The music was composed by Isaac Dunaevsky (1900–1955) and the lyrics were written by Vasily Lebedev-Kumach (1898–1949). The chorus sings: "Wide is my Motherland, / Of her many forests, fields, and rivers! / I know of no other country / Where a man can breathe so freely."

4. See reference 1.

5. The Civil War (17 May 1918 – 19 June 1923 года) was sparked by the 1917 October Revolution, as many factions rivalled to determine Russia's political future.

6. The Great Patriotic War fought between the Soviet Union and Nazi Germany was a theatre of World War II (1 September 1939 – 2 September 1945) and lasted from 22 June 1941 to 9 May 1945.

7. The Volga German Autonomous Soviet Socialist Republic was created following the October Revolution, by a 29 October 1918 decree of the Soviet government, establishing the Labour Commune of Volga Germans. This gave Soviet Germans a special status among the non-Russians in the USSR. It was restructured as an Autonomous Soviet Socialist Republic on 20 February 1924. Its capital city was Engels (known as Pokrovsk or Kosakenstadt before 1931) located on the Volga River. Out of almost 2 million Germans living in the USSR the republic was home to 366,685 Germans (60.5% of the republic's population) according to the census of 1939. As a result of the German invasion of the Soviet Union in 1941, the republic was abolished and Volga Germans were exiled.

8. Federalnoye agentstvo po delam natsionalnostey.

9. Kapustin Yar ("cabbage ravine") is a Russian military training area and a rocket launch complex in Astrakhan Oblast, about 100 km east of Volgograd. On 3 June 1947 Kapustin Yar was designated as the location of the new rocket test site. Since the 1950s, 11 nuclear explosions have been conducted at the Kapustin Yar test site. From 1957 to 1961, five atmospheric nuclear tests were performed over the site. In addition to nuclear tests, 24,000 guided missiles were exploded in Kapustin Yar, 177 samples of military equipment were tested, and 619 intermediate-range ballistic missiles with nuclear warhead were destroyed. On 8 January 1992, during a trip to Saratov Oblast, President Boris Yeltsin made a statement on the issue of the restoration of the Volga German Autonomous Soviet Socialist Republic, proposing that Soviet Germans move to Kapustin Yar instead of their legitimate territory: "...and let this land, which is filled with shells, may they cultivate it... There may be some such region in some future and there will be, or there may be some such national Volga region Germans, but only when there will be 90 percent of Germans."

10. Federal'naya natsional'no-kul'turnaya avtonomiya "Rossiyskiye nemtsy".

11. Mezhdunarodnyy soyuz nemetskoy kul'tury.

© **AFZ ETHNOS e. V. Journal of Ethnic Microhistory**
Issue 12, II-2025

Editor: Dr. *(Inst. f. Orient.)* Walther Friesen

Layout Design and Cover Collage by Tatiana Friesen

Publisher: Dr. Walther Friesen on behalf of the registered association
Training and Research Center ETHNOS / Ausbildungs- und Forschungszentrum ETHNOS e.V.

Reference Address: Bermesdickerstr. 9, 44357 Dortmund, Germany
Tel.: +49 231/317 30 20
E-Mail: afz.ethnos@gmail.com

AFZ ETHNOS e.V.

DORTMUND 2025

Publisher: BoD · Books on Demand GmbH, Überseering 33,
22297 Hamburg, bod@bod.de
Print: Libri Plureos GmbH, Friedensallee 273, 22763 Hamburg

ISSN 2749-9685　　　　　　　　　　**ISBN 978-3-8192-3067-7**